TRIAL OF
ELVIRA BARNEY

CELEBRATED TRIALS SERIES
GENERAL EDITOR: JONATHAN GOODMAN

CELEBRATED TRIALS

TRIAL OF ELVIRA BARNEY

With an Introduction
and Edited by

PETER COTES

DAVID & CHARLES
NEWTON ABBOT LONDON
NORTH POMFRET (VT) VANCOUVER

This book is dedicated to Joan Miller,
wife—actress—fellow addict,
With love

ISBN 0 7153 7294 7

Library of Congress Catalog Card Number 76-45510

Set in 11 on 12pt Linotype Baskerville and printed in
Great Britain by Latimer Trend & Company Ltd Plymouth
for David & Charles (Publishers) Limited
Brunel House   Newton Abbot   Devon

Published in the United States of America
by David & Charles Inc
North Pomfret   Vermont 05053   USA

Published in Canada
by Douglas David & Charles Limited
1875 Welch Street   North Vancouver   BC

CONTENTS

Third Day

EDITOR'S NOTE

Down the years I have known many who knew Elvira Barney. With such information as I have been supplied by these mutual acquaintances, a few of them personal friends of mine, I may have been helped to write more about Elvira than has appeared in earlier essays on the case. Much of this account must be my own presumption, based upon facts and the sifting of evidence from several sources. Some of it is hearsay; but, as was so in the trial itself, not all hearsay evidence need automatically be excluded. The report of the court proceedings over the three days speaks for itself. Such 'background' as I have been able to supply to the tragic events in the early hours of 31 May 1932 could conceivably help in forming a detached opinion of the 'barney' in a small mews flat, between two world wars, that wrecked a cult and rocked a nation.

One way and another, Elvira Barney has been cropping up in my life since the time when, as a very young actor (in Charles B. Cochran's production of Noël Coward's *Cavalcade* at Drury Lane), I was first made aware of her through the evening newspapers I would regularly take into the dressing room. I have often wondered since whether Noël Coward read about her, too, and decided to call one of his best-known characters after the woman with the unusual name who proved to be such a great 'attraction' during her rather limited run at the Old Bailey.

Later I was to meet two of the three daughters of Elvira's defending counsel, one of whom I got to know well; and later the great man himself when, lunching at the Ritz in the late 1940s at the invitation of Philip Barry, whose play *The Animal Kingdom* I had just directed in the West End, my host invited 'Pat' Hastings, who was also a playwright, to join us for a liqueur.

Later still, in rapid succession, I was to meet three further members of the cast of that Old Bailey 'production'. First there was Arthur Jeffress, with whom my wife and I shared a day at the home of a mutual friend, Beverley Nichols, and later a dinner at our own home in Chelsea after we had driven him back to London from Surrey. During the day we had heard a little about Elvira, and I guessed when we invited him in for a drink that later, if he stayed to dine (which he invited himself to do), we should hear more. He was, as I remember him, both witty and wistful and, as befitted the last person but one to see Michael Stephen alive, a mine of information about the fateful night at Williams Mews. It was a pity we never saw Arthur Jeffress again. Like his friend Elvira, he was to die in Paris—not long after leaving us, but over a score of years later than her. Unlike her, he died by his own hand.

Then there was the trial judge. In 1951 I directed a drama-tisation of the Tennyson Jesse novel, *A Pin to See the Peep-show*, which dealt with the Thompson–Bywaters case, and the elderly, though still alert, Sir Travers Humphreys accepted my invitation to honour a matinee performance with his presence. He had been junior counsel for the Crown in Rex v Thompson and Bywaters (1923). After the performance, over tea, he expressed his fascination at having seen the Edith Thompson story re-enacted, and subsequently penned a con-gratulatory letter, which I proudly pinned on to the backstage notice-board for the benefit of the cast.

Subsequently I made the acquaintance of Judge H. C. Leon, better known to the reading public as Henry Cecil. But although Judge Leon as a young barrister attended the Barney trial 'upon behalf of an interested party', I never inquired who the interested party was. I have an idea, too, that such a query would have produced no satisfactory reply from a lawyer who, even when he sometimes poked good-natured fun at certain comical aspects of the law, would have regarded the identity of his 'interested party' as some sacred trust, to be treated in the strictest professional con-fidence.

On the night the Barney trial ended I went, together with

several other members of my dressing room at Drury Lane, to a small drinking club that was then open for after-the-show refreshments in a cellar in Gerrard Street, off Piccadilly Circus. It was called by the somewhat exotic name of 'Smokie Joe's', and I had made its acquaintance through its proximity to both the London Hippodrome and the Queen's Theatre, where I had recently played.

Shortly after midnight, down the steps clattered a trio—two women and a man—who immediately ordered drinks. There was a heaviness about the jowl and a tired brightness in the eyes of one of the women in the party that made her face appear familiar. But the lighting was subdued and it was not until later, when she unexpectedly lurched over to our table and, with what passed for a flashing smile, invited me to dance with her, that I knew for certain who she was. We danced, or rather walked, to a blues, and after a few minutes round that little dance floor I felt very tired indeed. The solitary jazz pianist finished his number and I remember (there are some things you simply cannot forget) that Elvira staggered back to her table, calling over her shoulder for me to join her party. But I went home to bed. I shall never know what prompted her gesture; nor shall I forget it. As I recall the memory of that brief early-morning encounter, made less distant as I write, it would seem, upon reflection, that Elvira Barney danced no better than she shot.

INTRODUCTION

Why shouldn't I have fun? I died young, didn't I?
'Elvira' in Noël Coward's *Blithe Spirit*

On 1 June 1932 the following brief report appeared, inconspicuously featured, on an inside page of a London newspaper:

TRAGEDY AFTER A COCKTAIL PARTY

Michael Stephen, the handsome son of a distinguished father, was found lying dead with a wound in his chest on the landing of an exotically furnished little house in Williams Mews, Lowndes Square, Knightsbridge, while Mrs Elvira Dolores Barney, the beautiful daughter of Sir John and Lady Mullens, stood distractedly above him, moaning and sobbing.

The tragedy has presented the police with a difficult and delicate problem. It is understood that their investigations have not established how the fatal shot came to be fired. It is probable that further investigation will be left to the coroner and his jury, who will have to decide in what way the young man met his death.

This was to be followed three days later by a front-page item that read:

Mrs Elvira Dolores Barney, the beautiful daughter of Sir John and Lady Mullens, was arrested last night in the house of her parents in Belgrave Square, S.W.

She was taken to Gerald Road police station and charged with the murder of Mr Michael Scott Stephen, who was found shot dead on Tuesday morning.

When Mrs Barney appeared at Westminster Police Court on 6 June charged with murder, it was merely to hear evidence of formal arrest. Her reply to the charge was, 'I did not shoot him. I am not guilty.'

From these initially bare reports was to emerge a murder

trial such as had not been before the courts for years, according to Mrs Barney's counsel, Sir Patrick Hastings. It was certainly 'the murder of the year'; the most vivid and controversial; the most theatrical because it was the most dramatic. Its worldwide audience had no difficulty in appreciating its topicality, for outside that period in time perhaps the very events that stirred so many to debate the character of the woman on trial for her life would never have happened. Julian Symons has written in *Between the Wars*:

> In retrospect the whole period looks like an interregnum between the savage realities of two wars, but again, of course, it was not like that for those who lived through it. The pictures as one turns them over are optimistic, sad, nostalgic, unbelievable. Were there actually Bright Young Things?

'There was a terrible barney at No 21', neighbours told the police after the shooting, using the word in the sense of a rowdy jollification and without being conscious of the pun. It was Elvira's party that caused it, of course; that was what the barney was all about. Such parties were dangerous: lavish but sleazy, and often frequented by drug-takers. In those days you had to be a member of a select coterie to get the 'stuff'. At one such party, held in a house in Chelsea Church Street a short time earlier and attended by Elvira, a young man named Philip Carew had hurled himself out of a top-floor window while 'high' on cocaine. He was dead when they found him. His death caused no widespread comment, few questions. Pushing and taking dope was rarely seen by bystanders, as it is today, in public lavatories, at hippie carnivals, and outside West End chemists, when the sight of addicts fixing themselves, and sometimes selling the stuff to anyone whose needs—or finances—are greater than their own, provides a gruesome spectacle. At the time of the Barney case such things were not done publicly; drug-taking was an activity reserved for private gatherings.

The type of party favoured by Elvira Barney was only one of many given by the rich. In the squares of St James, Belgrave, Portman, Grosvenor and Berkeley the glittering parties were thrown by and for the mighty of the land. And some of the children of the mighty concocted novel party formats: there were circus parties, pyjama and nightdress parties, Swiss/Greek/Russian parties, Royal Flying Corps/nautical/marine parties, fireworks parties, bathing parties, adults-dressed-as-kiddies parties; for a Mozart party given by David Tennant, the bill came to over £3,000, which in today's accounting—with service *and* VAT—could well amount to ten times that figure. One wonders what the unemployed and the destitute thought about such extravagance.

It is doubtful whether Elvira Barney ever thought about what anybody, irrespective of class, thought of anything or anybody. She seems to have believed that her riches meant that she could afford to be selfish; she wanted her own way and was usually able to get it.

She was the elder, by three years, of two sisters. In October 1925 the younger sister, Avril, then only sixteen, married Prince George Imeretinsky, a member of a noble White Russian family. The wedding was held at St Margaret's, Westminster; the bride received from her father a flat in the then still exclusive Park Lane, a settlement of £4,000 a year, and a string of individually expensive pearls.

Sir John Ashley Mullens had been created a knight a few years before Avril's wedding. An Old Etonian, he was a trustee of the Stock Exchange and held the position of Chief Government Broker. The tall and striking Lady Mullens was said, with some justification, to look as young as her two daughters. In the 1920s and early 1930s, before the distressing events in which the whole family became helpless participants, the Mullens did much entertaining at their sumptuous town residence, 6 Belgrave Square, and at their country estate, the Manor House at Haslemere.

When Avril won her Prince, Elvira, who had been receiving stage training at Lady Benson's Acting Academy for some months past, decided to turn what was perhaps a teenage whim and an amateurish exercise into a rather more professional pursuit. Hence her appearance in *The Blue Kitten*, which opened at the Gaiety Theatre in the West End on 23 December 1925. The programme did not list the young

'Dolores Ashley' (she had taken both her own and her father's second Christian names as a theatrical pseudonym), but she is said to have been 'a pleasant kid, from what I remember of her' by a member of the cast, whose memory, though blurred, still recalls her polite manner and the pre-production publicity that resulted from the theatrical début, though in a tiny part, of the eldest daughter of such influential social lights as the Mullens.

Apparently, at the end of the run of *The Blue Kitten*, it was decided that Elvira was to return to the conventional life of a well-bred and well-heeled young woman. She was seen at first nights, smart restaurants and royal garden parties. She engaged in the social round of hunt balls, Henley, Ascot, Goodwood, the Eton and Harrow match at Lords, and week-end shooting parties. She helped her mother entertain throughout the year and especially during the 'season' at the fine London house.

Late in 1927, at one of the gatherings at 6 Belgrave Square, she first met the man she was destined to marry. John Sterling Barney was an American entertainer who had appeared in the revue *Many Happy Returns* at the Duke of York's Theatre, and had played in cabaret and on the music-hall stage in a singing act, 'The Three New Yorkers'. It was a good little trio—top–hat–white–tie–and–tails in style—and Barney's partners were later to continue as a double act under the name of Ross and Sergeant, becoming well-known in cabaret and on gramophone records. 'The Three New Yorkers' were popular entertainers at society functions, and after they had performed their act at a party given by Lady Mullens, Barney danced with Elvira, who seems to have at once succumbed to his facile charm. They arranged to meet again, and before long a close relationship developed. On 2 August 1928 they were married at Princes Row Register Office, a venue which, in comparison with St Margaret's, Westminster, suggests that the Mullenses questioned whether it was a fair exchange to lose Elvira as a daughter and gain John Sterling Barney as a son.

The marriage was a failure from the start. At the trial Sir Patrick Hastings referred to Barney as a 'brute'. Although no evidence was produced to substantiate this description, it seems to be confirmed by the recollection of Effie Leigh, one of Elvira's friends, and the only person, apart from Lady Mullens, whom she wished to see while awaiting trial in Holloway Prison: 'One day she held her arms in the air, and the burns she displayed—there and elsewhere—were, she insisted, the work of a husband who had delighted in crushing his lighted cigarettes out from time to time on her bare skin.'

The violent rows started in earnest within weeks of the marriage. A few months later the cabaret artist left Elvira and returned to the United States; 'the beautiful blonde', who was to go so quickly to seed, and the singing American, who had so quickly stopped singing, never saw each other again. (Four years later, his wife about to stand trial, Barney was to send a cable to Lady Mullens; apart from a brief news-paper paragraph later still, this was the last to be heard of the former member of 'The Three New Yorkers'.)

After the parting Elvira's life-style grew even more rackety. She started 'sniffing the snow', along with Brenda Dean Paul's set, whose kicks came from a wide variety of drugs. She threw parties, frequented night clubs and bars, and became the demanding but generous mistress of a number of disorient-ated and sexually odd lovers. After a succession of such affairs she was to be found at the start of 1932 living with Michael Scott Stephen, a good-looking man of twenty-five who described himself as a dress-designer.

If Stephen appeared more worthless than Elvira, it was only because she was rich and he was not. His father, the London manager of the North of Scotland Bank and a Justice of the Peace, had grown so disgusted with his son's mode of living that he had cut off a private allowance and barred him from the family home; his mother, however, continued to send him small sums of money. There were two other brothers and a sister. All three sons had been educated at Shrewsbury; Stephen's sister, in 1932, was studying domestic science.

Stephen shared Elvira's banking account as well as her bed, at 21 Williams Mews, which had been a garage before being converted into a four-roomed maisonette. The Mews itself was a narrow cobble-paved cul-de-sac leading off the Knightsbridge end of Lowndes Square, and was mainly comprised of stables and garages with living quarters above them for chauffeurs and their families.

Whether Elvira derived most pleasure from the dope, the alcohol or the wild parties is anybody's guess. Whether she experienced a vicarious thrill from her lover's activities with other men, which were additional to his heterosexual behaviour with her, cannot be ascertained at this late date. What we can accept, in the light of subsequent disclosures, is that much of the fighting and screaming that went on between them was produced to whet the appetite of each partner in what was a perverse sexual relationship. But however odd their liaison, there is no doubt of Michael's contentment in being kept and Elvira's contentment in keeping him. 'I was more in love with him than with any of the others', she was to say later. Many of her remarks must be viewed with suspicion, but not this one.

The day and night of Monday, 30 May 1932, proceeded in a manner that was more or less normal, if one can apply that word to such a relationship. Elvira and Michael lunched in the West End after staying in bed until nearly noon, sleeping off the effects of a party; more drinks were consumed before, during and after their meal. Then they returned to Williams Mews to prepare for the party they were giving that night.

From about six o'clock until past ten a babble of voices and the strains of jazz records sounded through the open windows; cars of the open-carburetter type, fast and noisy mechanical monsters in lurid colours, came and went. If the time passed quickly for the party-goers, it must have dragged for the neighbours. However, Elvira's last party at 21 Williams Mews was allowed to run its course: on earlier occasions during the year or so she had lived in the Mews some of the chauffeurs and their wives had called in the police to stop the pandemonium, but there were no interruptions tonight.

According to Arthur Jeffress, the last arrival, he stayed on and accompanied Elvira and Michael to the Café de Paris for 'supper' and then to the Blue Angel Club in Soho for drinks. It was after 2 am when they left Jeffress and returned home. He said later that they had *appeared* to be friendly.

At about 4.40 am the telephone rang at the home of Dr Thomas Durrant, a well-known West End physician, who had attended Mrs Barney for certain maladies whose nature was never disclosed. Crying hysterically, Mrs Barney said that there had been a terrible accident at 21 Williams Mews, and begged the doctor's wife, who had answered the call, to get her husband to come at once. A few minutes later the telephone rang again. Mrs Barney, sounding more incoherent than ever, was now demanding to know why the doctor had not already arrived. Dr Durrant arrived at the maisonette, in fact, less than 10 minutes later, but by that time Stephen was dead. He was lying on the stairs, shot in the chest at short range. Elvira was sobbing and screaming in turn, incoherently moaning and kissing the dead man. She kept repeating: 'He wanted to see you to tell you it was only an accident.'

The doctor called the police, who arrived within a few minutes. Despite her hysteria and dazed condition, the story Mrs Barney told the first officers on the scene was the same that she was to tell throughout the subsequent interrogations. In bare outline it was that when she and Michael had returned from the night club and gone to bed, an argument had started. He had got out of bed, threatened to walk out on her and dressed with the intention of doing so. There had been an argument about a revolver that Elvira kept on the premises and Michael was taking with him. He left the bedroom with it and she followed in an attempt to regain the weapon. There was a struggle, during which Michael was accidentally shot.

Sir John and Lady Mullens were telephoned. The police, anxious to question Elvira further, made preparations to take her to the police station before her parents arrived. What was left of her self-control snapped and she slapped the officers' faces, struggled as they tried to hold her and threatened them with dire consequences if they put her in a cell. 'You foul

B

swine', she screamed at one of the detectives. 'Now you know who my mother is, perhaps you will be more careful what you say and do to me.'

It is a curious aspect of the case that the police did little or nothing to restrain Elvira in the face of great provocation, though a violent attack upon any of their number, especially under the shadow of what was suspiciously akin to previous violence resulting in death, should have been sufficient reason for doing so. What is more surprising is that, immediately after making her statement at the police station, she was allowed her liberty *unconditionally*. The police may have felt that their suspicions were not strong enough to justify a charge being preferred; even so, a woman suffering such strain and having already displayed violence in their presence might surely have been regarded as too dangerous to be let loose at that time.

Elvira Barney made three statements within a few hours of the shooting, but as they hardly differ, we shall concentrate on one only, which reads as follows:

I am twenty-seven years of age and of no occupation. I have been residing at the above address alone for about a year. I am a married woman living apart from my husband who is at present in America. The last I heard of him he was a singer. He left me about two-and-a-half years ago. I have known a man named Michael Scott Stephen for about a year. I was introduced to him through friends.

We were great friends and he used to come and see me from time to time. He had no occupation. He always used to see me home and last night he did so as usual. We arrived home at 2 am. Immediately we got in we had a quarrel about a woman he was fond of. He knew I had a revolver in the house. I have had it for years. I do not know where it came from. It was kept in various places. Last night it was under the cushion of a chair in the bedroom, near the bed. I was afraid of it and I used to hide it from time to time. He knew where it was last night. He took it from under the chair saying, 'I'm going to take it away for fear you will kill yourself.' He went into the room on the left. I ran after him and tried to get it back. There was no struggle in the bedroom. He was outside in the spare room in the doorway. As we were struggling together—he wanted to take it away and I wanted to get it back—it went off. Our hands were together, his hands in mine, for a few minutes. I did not think anything had happened. It seemed quite all right.

I did not think anything serious. He went into the bathroom and half shut the door. He said, 'Fetch a doctor.' I asked, 'Do you really mean it?' I did not have the revolver then. I think it had fallen to the ground.

I saw he looked ill. I rang up the doctor and no one answered. I went upstairs and saw him sitting on the floor. I was upset and began to cry. I again rang up the doctor and he said he would come. I went upstairs again. Stephen said, 'Why does not the doctor come? I want to tell him what has happened. It was not your fault.' He repeated that over and over again. I tried to cut his tie off. I put a towel on his chest and got pillows. I again rang up the doctor and they said he was leaving. I again went upstairs and saw he was dead and just waited. I don't remember what I did afterwards, I was so frantic. I am sure, as far as I know, there was only one shot fired.

Stephen and I had quarrelled on previous occasions, but not often,

(Signed) ELVIRA DOLORES BARNEY

31.5.32

After making the statement, Elvira went to her parents' house, where she was put to bed and heavily sedated.

During the rest of that day and the following one there was much police activity at 21 Williams Mews—and, for that matter, in the mews itself. Before long, items of information began coming in from many quarters – reports from forensic experts, and statements from neighbours and from acquaintances of Elvira and Stephen. But there was silence from most of those who had attended the party. Arthur Jeffress, the last person but one to see Stephen alive, was interviewed, and a statement was taken from Hugh Wade, who had been at the party and later played the piano at the club where Elvira, Jeffress and Stephen had finished up their night with drinks. The rest of the party-goers were bashful about coming forward. One man telephoned but was not prepared to give his name; he arranged to meet the police but failed to turn up.

The tenants of the mews were agog with excitement. A man had been shot by one of their number, and they knew more about it than anybody else. Some of them claimed that they had heard not only the noise of the quarrel, but Mrs Barney shrieking, 'I will shoot you'. Some of them insisted that there had been more than one shot. (There was apparent corroboration of this from the fact that two chambers of the five-chambered pistol had been fired, and the mark of a second bullet had been found by the police in the wall where the stairs turned.) Some people living a good distance from No 21 claimed to have heard a quarrel on a previous night. Stephen, they said, had walked out of the maisonette and Elvira had leaned out of a window, screaming, 'Laugh, baby, laugh for the last time', and then produced a gun and fired at him.

It seemed to the police that statements like these—coupled with information contained in the preliminary reports of Sir Bernard Spilsbury, the pathologist, and Robert Churchill, the gunsmith—provided adequate evidence for charging Mrs Barney with murder. She was arrested four days after the shooting and brought before Mr Boyd, the magistrate at Westminster Police Court.

Her first appearance only served the purpose of ensuring that she would have expert legal representation. Walter Frampton, one of the most able criminal lawyers of his day, represented her at the second police court appearance, when she was bound over for a further week. The police utilised the time to complete their case and make Elvira's committal a foregone conclusion. Sir John and Lady Mullens took the opportunity to prevail upon a reluctant Sir Patrick Hastings to lead Frampton in the defence. She was fortunate in this respect, if in little else.

The only recollection of the police court proceedings to stay in Sir Patrick's memory was Elvira's appearance. She was less composed than at any other time since her arrest, and her face was ashen pale. Although described as a beautiful member of a smart set, she was anything but beautiful now; her mode of life in recent years had coarsened her looks. Her present ordeal was doubtless a contributory factor in determining her counsel's verdict on her lack of charm. He said in his autobiography:

> My first view of Mrs Barney was slightly depressing . . . her appearance was not calculated to move the hearts of a jury; indeed she was a melancholy and somewhat depressing figure as she stood in the dock with a wardress upon each side of her.

But if the memory of Sir Patrick remained clear about his client in his autobiography, he was less sure about his own part when cross-examining those two star witnesses, Sir Bernard Spilsbury and Robert Churchill; the former the Home Office's most distinguished pathologist, and the latter a firearms expert. When both cast doubts on the prisoner's version of the shooting, Sir Patrick had to break his own rule that it is better not to cross-examine in a police court when the criminal charge is a serious one. This rule was based on his belief that the barrister, when engaged for the defence in a capital charge that was almost certain to be sent to a higher court, should act as an observer, the silent friend at court, holding a watching brief rather than behaving as an active advocate. Writing about the case, Sir Patrick recalled: 'The proceedings in the police court were not unduly prolonged as there was no cross-examination.' But memory played him false. He did, in fact, examine witnesses, including Spilsbury, and gave the latter a foretaste of the type of long and searching cross-examination to which he might be subjected later on. There was more than one sharp passage of words, and when Spilsbury attempted to qualify a statement regarding the likelihood of both Stephen's and Mrs Barney's hands being on the trigger of the gun when it went off, and refused to give Hastings an unqualified 'Yes' or 'No' reply, he was told: 'I will now ask you the same question over again. I would like you to answer my question, yes or no.' Spilsbury replied that perhaps he could put it another way, to which came the retort that counsel would rather he put it in *his* way.

So much for the great advocate's memory regarding the tactics to be employed at police court proceedings. His lapse here was less odd than when reading aloud one of Elvira's letters. He had got well into this before realising that it was the wrong one to read at that time:

> Michael darling, at last I have got your sweet little letter. It was not very long was it? If only I had received it last night I should have slept well. As it was I wondered if you really love me and it kept me awake all night.

This was part of a letter to be carefully noted by the magistrate, but at the trial it was never submitted as evidence. The only one of Elvira's 'passionate' letters that was to be read aloud then was the one in which her belief that Michael loved her was never in serious doubt.

The star performer of the Barney Case was, without a doubt, Sir Patrick Hastings. A man of the drama in the theatre (he had written a number of plays, none of them lucky enough to enjoy really long runs), he was the opposite of the old-style courtroom orator and fiery advocate. By the time the Barney Case arrived he was in his early fifties and at the height of his fame as a Kings Counsel. When he sat in court, a spare lithe intense figure, with arms folded and wig slightly tilted over his brow, his eyes looking ahead or occasionally glancing at the dome of the court, his gold pencil continually rolled by thin nervous fingers, it was he who attracted the most interest. He did not seek the audience and the applause; they came to him as if by natural right. He invariably held the centre of the stage.

This was the man whom Sir John Mullens begged to defend his daughter. Sir Patrick hesitated. He was up to his eyes in work, with more than a score of heavily marked briefs in his chambers. Apart from the demands on his time, there was his well-known dislike of participating in trials involving a capital charge. It was said later by his daughter Patricia that his sole reason for accepting this particular case was his wife's persuasiveness. There had been a curious, though remote, link some years earlier when by coincidence the Hastings children had had a governess who had formerly been in the employ of Sir John and Lady Mullens. The governess had called her former charge 'dear little Elvira', and Lady Hastings, remembering this term of endearment when she read about the arrest, felt acutely distressed for the parents of such a paragon. It was highly providential for 'little Elvira' that the wife of the man who was to plead her case so brilliantly remembered her as such.

From the start the case was treated on a highly emotional level—a melodramatic approach by the press, and purple passages galore:

> The door of the police court opened to admit a Mrs Barney whose step was steady and gaze alert. Pale, perhaps, the rouged lips accentuating the pallor, yet with her emotions obviously under control. The hand of the matron rested lightly and guidingly upon one black swathed arm, but Mrs Barney gently but firmly released herself. She passed me so close that I heard her husky murmur, 'I can manage, thank you'. And before a well-meaning court official could reach her side, she passed into the dock, which is more like a gangway, and settled herself comfortably with her feet upon the lower rail. The tiny green bottle of smelling salts which was handed to her she dropped into her lap with a repeated, 'I am all right, thank you'. Then she looked across to Lady Mullens with the smile of a child who wishes to assure her mother that all is well with her. Occasionally she dabbed at her eyes and sometimes the shoulders shuddered, but she displayed no other emotion. There was no warning of the collapse which came at the end of an hour . . .

Michael's will was reported soon afterwards. It was very short, but anything to do with the case was compulsive reading, and when an evening newspaper printed the fact that '£5 was the sum left by Michael Stephen (real name William Scott Stephen) described as a dress designer, aged 25, whose address in his will was given as the Park Lane Hotel, Piccadilly, W.1.', it was as front-page news.

Voices were heard calling for the estranged husband. 'Where is John Barney?' demanded *The Daily Telegraph*. When he received news of Elvira's arrest, he suddenly left his New York apartment. Rumours started flying around that he was on his way to London, but even if he ever intended to stand by Elvira, he never arrived. His only reaction was to send two separate cables. The first, to Elvira, read: 'Petty squabbles are forgotten now'; and the second to Lady Mullens, 'Stand by and do everything for Elvira's defence.'

Special teams of reporters were assigned to analyse the leading players in the drama. 'A Woman Reporter' gave Elvira a close-up from the 'woman's angle'—sob-stuff that has rarely been equalled:

> A young woman sobbing. Her gold shingled hair grown so long that it straggles outside her smart hat . . . She is dressed in a simple black dress and coat and a close-fitting black hat encircled with a wreath of black and white camellias . . . Her shoulders twitch the whole time. Her fingers are nicely manicured and she wears on one of them a huge sapphire ring. Her face is dead pale, but she has used her lipstick before coming to the court . . . Everyone leans forward except the impersonal wardress and her charge, who appears to be slipping sideways off the bench. It is by those twitching shoulders and the angle of the head that you can see how the ordeal is telling upon her. The clothes of the dead man are being examined. At the sight of his coat and canary-coloured pullover, Mrs Barney bursts into sobs . . . The last witness has been called. Mrs Barney is asked to stand. She runs her fingers through her side curls, and as she is helped to her feet the contents of her handbag fall out, and coppers go spinning over the floor of the court. Then, supported by the wardress, she is led away . . .

The bare facts were that a woman accused of shooting her lover had been committed to stand her trial at the Old Bailey. Unfortunately 'bare facts', however dramatic, have rarely endeared themselves to popular newspapers, whose principal aim, in order to beat their nearest rival's circulation figure, seems to be to transform drama into melodrama. The press of the year 1932 had had murder in *low* places. Now it was to be murder in *high* places. As Edgar Lustgarten has said in *Defender's Triumph*:

> In contrast to the Borgias of fourteenth-century Italy and to the Medicis of sixteenth-century France, the well-to-do

classes of twentieth-century Britain did not go in for killing, except with motor cars . . . Its one great murder trial which did involve the rich came to many as a bolt out of the blue.

It is small wonder that large sections of the country looked forward to an exposure of high society as the trial drew near —an even bigger, better, more dramatic *crime passionnel* than any of its predecessors down the years. Admittedly, there was then no television to take the scenes, described by a newscaster, into the sitting room; possibly the written word of the journalist who excelled in the 'purple passage' was superior in entertainment value. The morning and evening papers vied with each other in composing the most lurid banner headlines, and on the placards were to appear such appetising morsels as 'Love Hut Letters', 'Amazing Notes in Barney Case', 'Mrs Barney Sensation', 'Barney: More Revelations', and 'Elvira Collapses'.

The trial opened at the Central Criminal Court, Old Bailey, on 4 July 1932 before Mr Justice Humphreys, who was later to be described by Sir Patrick Hastings as almost, if not quite, the best criminal judge he had ever known. Sir Ernle Blackwell, Permanent Under Secretary at the Home Office, occupied a seat next to the Clerk of the Court, and the Director of Public Prosecutions, Sir Tindal Atkinson, was also in Court. Sir Percival Clarke and Mr L. A. Byrne appeared for the Prosecution; Sir Patrick Hastings, KC, Mr Walter Frampton, and Mr Maurice Alexander for the Defence.

Elvira's leading counsel had refused to see her before the trial, although she had sent several messages begging him to visit her in prison. Hastings says in his autobiography that his decision was based on his fear that he would be 'hampered in the conduct of her defence either by something the defendant may have said or by something she may have thought her counsel may have wished that she would say. I am afraid that Mrs Barney was disappointed at my refusal to see her.'

The Crown's case looked strong. Mrs Hall, a neighbour, had testified at the Police Court that before the fateful shot she heard Mrs Barney shouting, 'Get out, I'll shoot you.' The experts in the case, Sir Bernard Spilsbury and Robert

Churchill, had thrown serious doubts on the version that it was an accident; Churchill, the gunsmith, had described the weapon as one of the safest made and had spoken of the heavy pull of the trigger. It would be Hastings' task to shake the formidable battery of expert opinion and, if possible, discredit *those* who thought they had seen—and heard so much.

Sir Percival Clarke opened the case for the Crown fairly and with restraint. Warning the jury that unlawful killing was murder unless otherwise proved, he urged them to look for any evidence consistent with innocence that would permit them to know how Stephen could possibly have died by means other than the prisoner firing a pistol at him. He enumerated points that told against the prisoner, such as her unrestrained outburst against the police after the tragedy and her firing from the window of No 21 at Stephen when he was leaving about three weeks earlier.

The Crown's first witness was on the point of being called when Hastings rose to make an application to the Judge that all Crown witnesses should leave the Court until they were needed to give evidence. *Not* including Sir Bernard Spilsbury, the Judge's expression seemed to say—but what he was *heard* to say was, 'Including Sir Bernard Spilsbury?' and then, 'Be it so'. And out they all trooped.

The Crown's first witnesses dealt with routine matters: Stephen's brother with evidence of identification, the police with the finding of the body. They were followed by the two intimates—Jeffress and Wade—who had been present at the party and later at the Café de Paris and the Blue Angel. Then came the witness who lived opposite No 21, Mrs Hall, a chauffeur's wife, who told of watching the comings and goings at the cocktail party, of seeing Mrs Barney and her friends leave afterwards, and of hearing Mrs Barney screaming at four o'clock in the morning. 'I . . . heard Mrs Barney say she was going to shoot. She said it twice . . . I heard a shot . . . I heard Mr Stephen shout: "What have you done?" Mrs Barney was screaming out, "Chicken, come back to me; I will do anything I can for you." ' Mrs Hall went on to say that there had been some shooting about three weeks before. Mrs Barney had fired out of the window.

SIR PERCIVAL CLARKE: Where was Mr Stephen?—He was at her door talking and calling and asking her for money.

Did she give him any?—She told him to go and fish for it. Mr Stephen went away in the taxi cab in which he had arrived and then returned, walking. I saw Mr Stephen going away from the house, and Mrs Barney looked out of the window and said: 'Laugh, baby; laugh for the last time', and she fired.

How was she dressed?—I don't think she had anything on.

How do you know she fired?—I saw her and heard the shot.

Did you see in which hand she held the pistol?—The left.

Where was Mr Stephen standing?—Practically outside my door.

Did he appear to be hit?—No. He told Mrs Barney not to be so foolish as everybody was looking at them.

Did she go inside?—She fell as though she had fainted.

Where did Michael go?—He got into a greengrocer's van standing in the mews.

Have you heard quarrelling between them before?—Many times.

In his cross-examination, SIR PATRICK HASTINGS asked the witness:

Do you happen to know that the name by which Mrs Barney frequently addressed Stephen was Mickey?—It might have been.

Are you prepared to pledge your oath that the words she used were not 'Mickey, Mickey, don't leave me'?—I am quite sure the word she used was 'Chicken'.

If you are wrong about that, and the word was 'Mickey', do you think you are as likely to be wrong about anything else you heard?—I still say the word she used was 'Chicken'.

Mrs Kate Stevens, also a chauffeur's wife, who lived at No 8, was then called. She said that she had heard two shots fired, and then two more shots. By this time it was about half-past four. 'I went to bed again, and then I heard a final shot . . . much louder . . . It seemed to me from the bedroom.' She had heard Mrs Barney and Stephen quarrelling but did not recognise the man's voice at first; after the last shot she heard Stephen say, 'What made you do it?' and then Mrs

Barney say, 'Michael, Michael, come back. I love you.' The witness then repeated almost verbatim Mrs Hall's account of the previous shooting episode.

Dr Durrant, who had arrived before anybody else, in answer to Elvira's SOS over the telephone, confirmed that he had talked to the prisoner before she had had time to prepare any story that was untrue to suit her own ends. After taking the doctor through the telephone calls for help, his arrival and discovery of the body and the prisoner's behaviour throughout, Sir Patrick Hastings went on to ask: 'Did she appear to be passionately devoted to this dead man?'

> DR DURRANT: Oh, yes.
> HASTINGS: Did she kiss him after he was dead?
> DR DURRANT: Yes, several times.
> HASTINGS: And did her actions appear to you, so far as you could judge, to be absolutely sincere and genuine?
> DR DURRANT: Certainly.

At the end of the long day, a weary Mrs Barney—'I can still see her agonised face as she stood in the dock', her counsel was later to recall—was escorted down to the cells while the fashionable sightseers restarted their chattering as they made for the exits, many of them more concerned as to which smart summer frock they could wear for the second day of the entertainment than with the predicament of their 'friend'.

The first part of the police evidence on the opening of the second day was of a formal nature. Detective Inspector Winter described the scene when he arrived, the position of the corpse at the top of the stairs, the revolver's proximity to the dead man's hand, the state of the drawing-room with its dirty bottles and glasses.

After describing the statement that Mrs Barney made at the police station, the inspector read out two passionate love letters he had found at the flat. Then Hastings proceeded to reduce the impact of the two chauffeurs' wives' evidence regarding the earlier shooting incident:

> HASTINGS: As a result of your inquiries, can you tell me whether anyone complained to the police about an attempted murder in the mews about a fortnight previously? . . . Or a

report of any shooting? . . . No complaint of any sort or kind?

INSPECTOR: Not to the police.

The inspector admitted that no trace of any bullet marks in the mews had been found, despite a very thorough search.

HASTINGS: Was this revolver examined for fingerprints?
INSPECTOR: Yes.
HASTINGS: Was it found that the marks on it were so blurred that no fingerprints were decipherable except one?
INSPECTOR: That is so.
HASTINGS: Whose was that one?
INSPECTOR: That was mine.

The Defence was holding its own. But now it was the turn of the experts, and the most notable of them all, Sir Bernard Spilsbury, entered the witness box to answer Sir Percival Clarke's questions about the cause of death. Spilsbury said: 'The wound was $2\frac{3}{4}$in below the left collar bone and $\frac{3}{8}$in to the left of the middle line of the front of the body. It was horizontal from back to front.'

The famous pathologist was the least histrionic of witnesses. However, the clinical details, calmly spoken, for some reason seemed to tickle the 'smart set' present, and that evening Hastings was to confide to his daughter Patricia that he had never in all his experience witnessed such repulsive behaviour in a court of law.

Clarke asked Spilsbury about suicide, and his admission that at the post-mortem on Stephen he had had to take such a possibility into account.

SPILSBURY: Such a possibility did not appear to be a reasonable one. In the first place, the bullet had not been fired from close to the body in the sense of touching it, at any rate as is usual in suicide injuries; it was also unlike suicides in that the aim was at the chest instead of the heart. There was also an absence of any attempt to draw aside the clothing. These things rendered suicide very improbable.

Clarke handed the revolver to Spilsbury, who said that it had a long and heavy pull and was impossible to discharge if pointed at the left side of the chest of the person holding it.

(*Stephen had been shot in the left lung.*) Spilsbury said: 'With the wrist bent as it must be bent I could not get enough power to discharge the pistol off at all'.

Hastings got to his feet, and the moment that so many had been waiting for had arrived. The pathologist was asked three short technical questions on bone formation. They were casually put; the great expert was in fact treated like a first-year medical student, and then dismissed. That was all. Spilsbury left the box, Hastings sat down. A murmur of surprise and speculation went around the court, but was quickly silenced by an usher.

Next followed expert No 2, Robert Churchill, the gunsmith, to answer Sir Percival's questions concerning the type of weapon used. Churchill said that the weapon was of strong make, in good working order, with a strong trigger pull.

When he rose to cross-examine, Sir Patrick's response to this flat statement was to smile, point the weapon at the ceiling and pull the trigger over and over again. Someone jumped, and Sir Patrick reassuringly said, 'There's no danger.' This drew a laugh, the only one in the trial. Anyone who witnessed the 'demonstration' must have thought that even a child could have handled such a toy; the impression conveyed was that in any struggle the gun might have gone off. The expert's expression, as he watched the pantomime, was as tight as the gun was supposed to have been. He was about to step down when—apparently as an afterthought—Hastings casually continued:

HASTINGS: If two people were struggling to get possession of a revolver, and the pressure exerted was not strong enough to fire it at first, the cylinder might be turned around?

CHURCHILL: It might spin round.

HASTINGS: If the struggling persons are close and one has the revolver in her hand, and the other seizes the hand, it would go off?

CHURCHILL: It might.

HASTINGS: When the finger, not of the person killed, is on the trigger?

CHURCHILL (after a pause): Yes.

This evidence concluded the case for the Prosecution. The

Defence then called a Crown witness, Dr Morton, the Governor and Medical Officer of Holloway Prison, who had examined Mrs Barney after her admission. He stated that he had found bruises on the prisoner, and agreed that they could have been caused during the alleged struggle over the revolver. Sir Patrick's next question was to help dispel rumour: 'Has there been, while the prisoner has been under your charge, the slightest indication that she has ever been addicted to drugs?' Dr Morton answered 'No'.

Then Sir Patrick quietly called the prisoner at the bar. Without hesitation Elvira walked almost languidly to the witness box, accompanied by the two wardresses who had been her constant companions in the dock for the last day and a half. Although only twenty-six, she looked at least twice her age—a raddled woman in her fifties. It was difficult to believe that only a few short years ago she had been appearing on the stage at the Gaiety Theatre, more for her physical appearance and position in society than for her histrionic ability. The courtroom was hushed as she replied to the first questions gently put to her by her counsel. The failure of a short marriage, the ill-treatment suffered at her husband's hands, her loneliness before taking a lease of the house in the mews, the relationship with Stephen, her wish to marry him as soon as she could get a divorce from John Barney.

Elvira's voice trembled several times at the start of the examination, and the Judge told her that she could sit. Her counsel watched patiently, making no attempt to hurry the examination. When he addressed her, his voice was soft and sympathetic.

HASTINGS: Had Stephen any means, so far as you know, of earning his living?
MRS BARNEY: No.

She agreed, in answer to Sir Patrick's questions, that she became very devoted to Stephen, was anxious to marry him, and supported him almost entirely. He was not always kind to her; she was sometimes frightened of him, on one occasion so much so that she called the police.

When Stephen came to your window in May and asked for money, what did you say or do?—He stayed outside the house for some time.

Do you remember what you did?—I was so unhappy that I thought I would make him think I was going to commit suicide. I got the revolver and fired at random. I thought he would think I had killed myself, and would fetch people, the police possibly, so I looked out of the window and he saw me and realised, I suppose, that I was all right and nothing more was said or done at the time.

On the left wall of your bedroom are the marks of a revolver bullet. When were they made?—On that occasion.

Was that the only occasion you fired the revolver before the day of Stephen's death?—Yes.

Then, as though it was the most easily answered query in the world, she was asked detail by detail about their return home to the flat that night.

I am afraid you must tell us this, Mrs Barney. Where did you go when you came back to the flat?—We went into the bedroom.

And at first, while you were in your room, was Michael Stephen kind to you, or was he not?—First of all, yes.

And what happened after you had been there for some time? Did he continue kind? Just tell us what he said to show how he changed.—He made love to me but was very angry because I did not respond in the way he wanted, and he said perhaps my feelings had changed. I told him that it was only because I was so unhappy at what had happened during the day – about money – and I could not forget it. That made him all the more angry. He said he was not pleased with the way things were going, and he wanted to go out the next day and not see me at all.

In other words, he was not either loving or kind at that time?—No.

What did Stephen do—did he stop in bed or get up?—He got up after some time. He dressed. I asked him not to leave me. I said if he did I should kill myself.

When you said you would kill yourself, did he say or do anything?—Yes, he got up from the dressing-table and made a dash for the armchair, and said: 'Well, anyway, you won't do it with this.'

Do you know how he knew the revolver was there?—I don't know exactly how, but he knew everything.

When he said: 'You won't do it with this,' what did he do?—He picked up the revolver. He ran out of the room towards the spare room. I ran after him.

At that time in whose hand was the revolver?—Michael's.

Did you come up to him?—Yes. In the doorway of the spare room.

Will you now tell us as much as you can remember of what then happened?—We struggled with the revolver. He had it and I wanted it back. I kept saying: 'Give it to me.' I don't know whether he said, 'No', but the more I tried, the more he tried to get it away. The struggle became more and more hard. We were moving about. I cannot remember all our positions. I was so unhappy. I was crying. I don't remember, but I know we were struggling and suddenly I heard a shot.

Stop there. Have you ever in your life desired to shoot Michael Stephen?—Never.

Has there ever been in your life anybody you were fonder of than Michael Stephen?—Never.

Did you shoot him that night?—No.

Had you any motive for shooting him?—None.

In his cross-examination Sir Percival Clarke strongly suggested jealousy as a motive for the shooting. This was the first suggestion of that emotion and Elvira looked surprised at the line of questioning, though agreeing without hesitation that there *was* another woman.

Sir Percival went in for the prepared 'kill', suggesting that she was consumed with jealousy of that other woman. No, Elvira replied wearily, the rows had been about gambling and not about sex. Later, in reply to Sir Percival's question: 'Did you say: "Get out, I'll shoot you"?' (which elicited a protest from the Defence that the words were, in fact, 'I'll shoot'), Mrs Barney stated that what she actually said was, 'Don't leave me, don't leave me. If you do, I'll shoot myself.'

Sir Patrick rose to re-examine. He studied the prisoner, nearly at the end of her tether in the witness box, and told her to stand, then asked that the pistol be placed on the ledge of the witness box. For a moment or two, it seemed an

c

eternity, there was silence. Hastings turned slightly away, then wheeled rapidly round to suddenly thunder: 'Pick up that revolver, Mrs Barney!' She picked it up—spontaneously —with her *right* hand. 'Have you ever picked up a revolver with your left hand in your life?' 'No', replied Mrs Barney. Not a soul in the court failed to realise that the prisoner had been taken by surprise and had acted without forethought; not a soul in the court failed to remember that Mrs Hall had sworn on oath that she saw the prisoner fire the revolver with her *left* hand.

Elvira's ordeal was over. The two stalwart wardresses helped her from the witness box back to the dock.

The Crown's final address was forcefully put by Sir Percival Clarke, who made great play with motive (jealousy) and the indications that the prisoner was a woman of uncontrollable temper. He pointed out that the hands of the dead man were clean, whereas they would surely have been blackened had he been holding the gun when it was fired.

The Judge refused the Defence application to make its *entire* speech before the Crown rose, and Sir Patrick therefore elected to commence his final address the next day.

After the court rose, Elvira's parents were again granted permission to visit their daughter in the cells below.

It was the second-act curtain for that highly theatrical audience, and as they exited, talking and laughing loudly, jostling and nudging each other, entering waiting cars, arranging where to meet that night—which party and at what time?—Pat Hastings surveyed the scene with ill-concealed loathing for those who had tried to turn a court of justice into a vulgar peepshow and peacock parade.

Immediately the court assembled for the last day, Sir Patrick was on his feet, laying about him with cutting scorn. It was the only emotion he displayed in what the Judge was later to term 'a remarkable forensic effort, certainly one of the finest speeches I have ever heard at the Bar'. Hastings flayed the sightseers and the curiosity-seekers; he showed his contempt in his manner as well as his words, referring to the strange amusement found by those who came to witness another person's agony. With more constraint, he scathingly referred to the Crown's contention that only 'slight provocation' had made his client strike a policeman.

Dispassionate but convincing, Elvira's defender spoke brilliantly and at length in his fight to save his client from the gallows. His closing speech was perfectly audible everywhere, but, being *pianissimo*, it could not command the applause of the laymen. In the years ahead it was to draw from the Bar itself many tributes, and Mr Justice Humphreys, who had sat grave and immobile throughout the address, was able, in summing-up, to tell the jury that the speech would assist them the more easily to reach the correct verdict because it had consisted of a careful analysis of the evidence and was free from anything like an appeal to sentiment.

After being out for two hours, the jury returned a verdict of Not Guilty. The Crown's decision not to press a further indictment (that of shooting at Stephen with intent to murder him or do him grievous bodily harm) was agreed to by the Judge. The woman who had been the prisoner at the Bar was one no longer; sobbing uncontrollably, she was resting her head on her arms, both supported by the dock's ledge. Meanwhile, Lady Mullens was being attended to by a physician, having collapsed on the floor as the Not Guilty verdict was being announced.

Apparently, before the Court rose, Sir Patrick Hastings made an application to the Judge regarding the prisoner's possession of firearms. There is no reference to this application in newspaper reports of the trial, but according to C. M. Rolph in *Living Twice*:

> Sir Patrick had planned his defence for a manslaughter verdict, and then the jury staggered him by declaring that Mrs Barney was not guilty of anything. The equally surprised Judge was about to discharge her when Sir Patrick, having recovered his breath and got to his feet said:
> 'My Lord, there remains one matter which it would be desirable to clear up. My client still faces the comparatively minor charge of possessing a firearm without a police certificate. If your Lordship would be so considerate as to—'
> 'Now, Sir Patrick,' said the Judge chidingly, 'I think you had better take further instructions.' And indeed his two

juniors were tugging at his gown to get him back into his seat
. . . The offence of possessing a firearm without a certificate
was not (then) an indictable offence, could not be dealt with
at the Old Bailey, and must be disposed of (as in due course
it was) by the magistrates.

In the streets outside, the news of the verdict spread
rapidly, and several hundred people were singing 'Three
Cheers for Mrs Barney' and 'For She's a Jolly Good Fellow'
as Sir Patrick Hastings unobtrusively left the Old Bailey.

C. H. Rolph, who, as Chief Inspector Hewitt of the City of
London police force, was on duty at the time, remembers the
occasion well: 'I was in Court throughout the trial and now
stood in the Judge's Corridor at the Old Bailey when the
court rose on the last day. As Mr Justice Humphreys passed
me, he said to his Clerk, "Most extraordinary! Apparently
we should have given her a pat on the back!"'

Elvira, although acquitted of murder by the jury, was
found guilty by the press of being loose, vicious and immoral.
A free press, we have been reminded, performs a vital role
in exposing wrongdoing and corruption. But a press that
becomes the public prosecutor rarely serves justice. Elvira's
life-style was played up for all it was worth; the implication
was that the company she kept was wholly appropriate to a
fortunate murderess.

Elvira joined that company while the tanks rumbled, the
dictators ranted and many people wondered where the next
meal was coming from. With 3 million unemployed, the
not-so-bright-young-things, left over from the twenties, were
still living a rainbow-coloured dream-life; they pursued their
idle lives with a relentless purpose that concealed its purpose-
lessness.

As Macdonald Hastings has pointed out in *The Other
Mr Churchill*:

Half of West End society smirked that it had been present
at the cocktail party which preceded the event, and the other
half were accused of it. In fact, it was attended by not more
than thirty people; and it is notable that there were as many
to risk their reputations as that. Elvira was rich and
generous; but her converted stable house hardly invited a

second visit. Even the police, when they saw the place, were as shocked as it is possible for policemen to be.

Over the cocktail bar in the corner of the sitting-room there was a wall painting which would have been a sensation in a brothel in Pompeii. The library was furnished with publications which could never have passed through His Majesty's Customs. The place was equipped with the impediments of fetishism and perversion. The revolver which killed Michael Scott Stephen, Mrs Barney's lover, may well have had a sexual association, too. There is reason to suppose that it wasn't the first time it had been fired.

But that is only one speculation among many in a case of which [Robert] Churchill's considered conclusion was: 'I never held that it was deliberate murder, but it was manslaughter and *sexually odd.*' The jury, at the trial, took a different view.

So many of the circumstances of the Mrs Barney affair are enveloped in question marks that, in reconsidering what her counsel, Sir Patrick Hastings, described in his autobiography as 'a murder in high life such as had not been before the Courts for years,' it is worth noting that even the bare account of the facts reveals, between the lines, that it was treated by the prosecution and the police with what might be regarded as the utmost, indeed almost inexplicable, restraint. Why, is anybody's guess.

When Dr Morton was asked whether he thought that Elvira was addicted to drugs, he answered 'No'. Probably all he meant was that he had found no syringe marks on her body. As stated previously, Elvira was a 'sniffer'; her addiction to cocaine bore no tell-tale signs. In cocaine addicts there is increased physical and mental power as part of the effect, and there may be perpetual disturbance and occasional paranoia. *Many addicts carry arms or weapons to respond to such stimulation.*

Michael Scott Stephen was most likely a pusher; we know for a fact that he was an addict. Beverley Nichols wrote: 'He was a very unpleasant little gigolo, who once offered me cocaine, which I threw back in his face.' And from a diary supposedly written by Stephen, excerpts from which were posthumously published in a popular Sunday newspaper a few days after the trial, it would appear that Mr Nichols's low opinion of Stephen was shared by Stephen himself:

> Women have loved me too much . . . I say this in no conceit, but rather with bitterness. It is just a plain statement of fact —women loved me too much. And how avaricious and all-demanding some of them can be. For many young men to be loved too much by women is bad—often fatal. Such love brings with it that worst of all curses—jealousy. Bright Young Things . . . I will say something of the *queer* slumming parties that we arranged, our ridiculous gambles, drugging sessions, the strange fashions that we initiated . . . I have played my sorry part in these affairs and will doubtless do so again. Sometimes I am happy and revel in the fun. But there are times when our way of life looks to me like one sickening round of illicit love, of furtive and shameless passion, jealousy, quarrels, drink and tragedy . . . I sometimes think that it is easier for the drug-addict to renounce his pet poison than for one of us to break away from this circle; easier for a prisoner to escape from behind stone walls and iron bars than for one of us to escape from this prison of the senses . . . But there were always cocktails to arouse a false sense of hilarity.

But what of the centre of this 'storm-in-a-court'? Elvira Barney was a woman of no importance who had been endowed with meretricious notoriety as the daughter of a rich and powerful father, the sister of a 'royal' and the recipient of a considerable family allowance. A good-time girl, cleared of murder after a brawl at her 'love nest' during which a gun had gone off, killing the man whose mistress she was, and leaving the Court in a state of collapse, she had sufficiently recovered by the following day to be photographed in a dozen different poses. And during that day she signed a contract with a Sunday newspaper for the publication of a series of articles. 'My Life' started with the words 'I write in tears', and was to continue in that vein for the better part of the two whole pages of its first instalment. But enough was enough, and after that first overlong splurge of miserable self-revelation, the newspaper and Elvira decided to throw in their hands and cancel what was to follow. If Elvira's 'Life' had continued as it had started, it would just have been another piece of unadulterated journalistic exhibitionism parading under the cover of a 'human document'.

After this, she spent much of her time abroad. It was in France that she very nearly killed the man who saved her from the gallows. Sir Patrick Hastings recalled in his autobiography:

> I saw her once more in my life . . . I was driving my car up the steep hill from Boulogne on the Paris road when a long low car driven by a woman, dashed round the corner on the wrong side, nearly killing me and my chauffeur who was sitting beside me. As he indignantly picked up his cap he said: 'Did you see who was driving that car, sir? It was Mrs Barney!'

Dr Johnson remarked that 'in human nature there is a general inclination to make people stare; and every wise man has himself to cure of it, and does cure himself'. Elvira, with her fast cars, bright-coloured clothes, promiscuous sex, wild parties, and emphatic nuisance value, never cured herself of wanting to 'make people stare'. This was an unfortunate trait in the character of 'dear little Elvira' from the time she started to play at amateur theatricals. It was to lead her into that brief flirtation with the professional theatre, far too disciplined in those days for her emotional instability, and finally into the midst of the Bright Young Things following the break-up of her marriage. She was a 'bawler' who, in a different stratum of society from that into which she was born, might have won for herself an award for the Best Billingsgate Fish Wife.

During the last years she changed her name: she wanted to forget, she said, that she was the notorious Mrs Barney. But she did little to change her mode of life—in Corfu, Majorca or Paris, or wherever else she went, with the Bairds, the Dean Pauls, Anna Wickham, and others who moved in her set. The same company, the same hobbies, all round the clock. She who shouted on the dance floor of the Café de Paris, 'I am the one who shot her lover—so take a good look' was the same woman who was to drink to excess and drive to

TO-DAY'S WEATHER: Fair and warm

131st Year.   No. 6,819.   JULY

MY LIFE STORY

And The Amazing Di

"I

MR

"L

MI

THE
to
ama
penn
figur
most
dies

MR
LIFE
·MY
STER

It i
Mrs. I
young
woma
Old B
dering
(" Mi
her 25
was f
Mrs.

Y MRS. BARNEY

Of "Michael" Stephen

**WRITING
TEARS"**

EY'S MEMORIES
HEARTACHE

ONE DEAD"

S VOICE FROM
GRAVE

atch"
two
ents
ding
the
rage-
nes:

OWN
SELF.
CHAEL "

o since
rney, a
society
at the
f
William
tephen,
who
in

the public danger. They found no 'gay' Elvira when they finally found her dead, but to the bitter end she was 'news'. The 'young blond boy', as they were to describe the elegant and effeminate young man named René Cady 'who proposed to her, had his plans cancelled and the ceremony postponed', gave interviews to the newspapers in the course of which he said that she was depressed by both the postponement and the lack of ready cash.

Elvira's last hours were true to form. Her end was a fitting conclusion to a theatrical play that had all the overtones of *grand guignol* and the undertones of a morality tale. She had, it appears, spent the early evening of Christmas Eve, 1936, in Montparnasse, the gay Latin Quarter where Mimis and Trilbys of Murger and du Maurier mingled with the exotic world that was Paris after dark. She went to the Coupole, the well-known Bohemian café, and later to the apartment of her more or less permanent escort, the said Monsieur Cady. While with friends at this flat, she insisted on listening to a midnight Mass broadcast from a Paris church. She was much affected by the singing, and cried bitterly. Her friends tried to cheer her up, and then all left for Montmartre. She was seen in several restaurants and cocktail bars, where she sat laughing and talking, surrounded by gaiety, cocktails and music. Sitting on a high stool at the bar, suddenly she fainted; and upon regaining consciousness, she said she felt ill and went back alone to her hotel. As she passed the night porter on the way to her room, she told him she felt very cold. He heard the key turn in her door.

M. Cady had arranged to see his fiancée on Christmas afternoon in his flat. When she did not come, he felt anxious, and with some of her friends went to her room. There was no answer to their knocking, and the door was broken in. They found her lying half on her bed and half off, fully dressed. There were signs of haemorrhage round her mouth. She had been dead many hours. Elvira was still clad in the black-and-white check dress and fur coat she had worn in Montmartre.

'She is a young woman with the rest of her life before her', her counsel had said at her trial. Four years later she was dead.

THE TRIAL

WITHIN THE

CENTRAL CRIMINAL COURT, OLD BAILEY, LONDON

Monday, 4 July 1932
and succeeding days

BEFORE

MR JUSTICE HUMPHREYS
(and a jury)

REX

against

ELVIRA DOLORES BARNEY

SIR PERCIVAL CLARKE and MR L. A. BYRNE appeared on behalf of the Crown (instructed by the Director of Public Prosecutions)

SIR PATRICK HASTINGS, KC, MR WALTER FRAMPTON, and MR MAURICE ALEXANDER appeared on behalf of the accused (instructed by Messrs Samuel Coleman, London)

CLERK OF THE COURT: Elvira Dolores Barney, you are charged that on 31 May last you murdered Thomas William Scott Stephen. How say you, are you guilty or not guilty?

THE PRISONER: Not guilty.

A jury was then empanelled and sworn.

CLERK OF THE COURT: Members of the jury. The prisoner at the Bar, Elvira Dolores Barney, is charged with the murder of Thomas William Scott Stephen on 31 May last. To this indictment she has pleaded not guilty, and it is your charge to say, having heard the evidence, whether she is guilty or not.

SIR PERCIVAL CLARKE *opened the case on behalf of the Crown*:

Mrs Barney is the wife of John Barney, whom she married nearly three years ago, and who, according to her story, left her a little more than two and a half years ago.

She has been living for the past eighteen months in premises known as Williams Mews, Lowndes Square—an extravagantly furnished converted flat on two floors. On the ground floor there was a lounge and a sitting-room, at one end of which was a cocktail bar. On the first floor there was a bedroom and another room, in which was a chair and a bath.

The man Stephen passed by the name of 'Michael'. He was a little younger than Mrs Barney—he was about 25—a young man of no occupation. So far as I know, when he did have any, it was that of a dress designer.

In the early hours of Tuesday, 31 May, a shot rang out in the upper part of those premises. Michael Stephen died. The only persons on the premises at the time were Mrs Barney and himself.

The question to which you will direct your attention is this: Was it Mrs Barney who caused his death? If it were, then she is guilty of murder, unless she did it in such circumstances as would reduce that crime in degree, or justify, or excuse. If she did not cause his death, you would find her not guilty of the offence charged against her.

On the night of Monday, 30 May, there was a cocktail

party at these premises, and Stephen served the cocktails. A large number of people attended—between twenty-five and thirty-five, I think—and from about seven until about nine or ten the party continued.

After the guests had gone, somewhere in the neighbour-hood of 10.30, Mrs Barney and Michael Stephen left to dine at the Café de Paris in Coventry Street.

There they were joined by Arthur Tilden Jeffress, who had known Mrs Barney for five years. He had known Stephen slightly for a much shorter period.

From the café the three went on to the Blue Angel Club, in Dean Street, Soho, where they joined a person who played the piano there, Hugh Wade, who had been one of the cocktail party.

They stayed until 12.30 or 1 am. From the time of their leaving until immediately before the shooting was heard, they were apparently together and alone at Williams Mews.

Between 4 am and 4.30 am screaming and shouting were heard from the first floor of Mrs Barney's premises. It was undoubtedly a quarrel between the two persons there, and Mrs Barney was heard saying: 'Get out, get out! I will shoot you! I will shoot you!' Stephen answered: 'I am going', and immediately there followed the report of a pistol. The next thing heard was in his voice: 'What have you done?' and from her, 'Chicken, chicken, come back to me. I will do any-thing you want me to.'

It was too late. The fatal shot had been fired. You will hear that within about ten minutes he must have died.

There was quiet for nearly a quarter of an hour, and then she was heard to call: 'Michael, Michael.' Then it was quiet again until the doctor arrived. By that time Michael was dead, and he died from the effect of a bullet wound through the left upper part of the lung. Mrs Barney had apparently rung on the telephone to Dr Durrant, who practises in West-bourne Grove, Paddington, for about 4.40 am his telephone bell rang. He had known Mrs Barney for a number of years. By the time the answer was made, the caller had gone.

Between three and four minutes to five, the bell rang again and this time the doctor answered it. Mrs Barney spoke, calling him at once to the mews and saying there had been a dreadful accident and that a man had shot himself.

At eight minutes past five, before he had left, the bell rang again, and the distraught voice of Mrs Barney called, 'Why haven't you come? Why aren't you here? Come at once. Jump into a taxi. He is bleeding. Come at once.' The doctor said he was coming at once, and at 5.14 started in his car. Mrs Barney met him at the door, and he will tell you her condition was one of hysteria.

On the landing he saw the dead man, reclining backwards on his left side against the wall, with his feet down the stairs, one straight and the other flexed. He was fully dressed. Dr Durrant noticed that the left arm was extended across the landing. The last three fingers of the left hand were flexed, and the other finger and thumb straight; outside the hand and at the back was a revolver, which will be a very cogent piece of evidence. His head was resting on pillows, which doubtless Mrs Barney had brought from the bed, and a towel had been pushed down inside his clothes to staunch the bleeding.

Mrs Barney was hysterical and overwrought; perhaps she realised what she had done. She was frenzied and said: 'He can't be dead. Why don't you do something for him? I love him so. I love him so.'

Then, although it was not a consecutive story she was telling, she expressed her feelings in a spasmodic effort. She said: 'It will kill my mother', and on another occasion said, 'I cannot live, let me kill myself.' To prevent any such idea from being put into execution, the doctor put his foot on the pistol. It was a very painful scene. She clutched the doctor, and when he said the police must be sent for, she said: 'Don't do that. You must not do that.'

The doctor tried to calm her and said: 'You have got to give me some account of what has happened.' To the best of his recollection, she told him they had quarrelled and that Michael had said he was going to leave her, and she had in some way indicated that she would commit suicide. Michael, knowing where the pistol was, picked it up from under the cushion of a chair and said: 'You won't do it with this.'

He was leaving the room when she closed with him,

wrestled and fought him. They got on to the landing and into the spare room, and the revolver went off. They separated. At first she did not know he was hurt. He went into the bathroom. She stayed outside calling, and then came a voice calling: 'Send for the doctor.'

The doctor pointed to a mark on the wall near the door where the plaster or the cement beneath the paper had been damaged by a bullet which had ricocheted into the wardrobe. She said: 'It was done some time ago.'

Her explanation as to having the revolver was that at times she was lonely, that there were quarrels between them, and that on some night before, when Stephen had made a disturbance outside and refused to go away, she had snatched up a revolver and fired at random. That was how the marks, she explained, were caused. Members of the jury, you will have to examine that with some care when you come to see the position of the marks on the wall and the hole in the furniture, which was built into the place and was made of cedar wood. While that was going on, Mrs Barney went down on her knees and passionately kissed Michael's body, expressing her deep love for him. Then the doctor's chauffeur brought back a police officer.

The police constable saw Dr Durrant on the landing and he sent for the divisional surgeon. He went down to the ground floor where Mrs Barney at that time was and she asked him: 'Is he dead?' The police officer said: 'I don't know.' She then said: 'I called the doctor and did my best for him.'

By 6.20 am Dr Arnold Harper, the divisional police surgeon, arrived. He examined the body and found that death had occurred, roughly speaking, about two hours earlier. There was found in the left lapel of the dead man's coat a small hole which might have been caused by the passage through the material of a bullet. There was blood on the pullover which Stephen was wearing beneath his coat and on the towel between the pullover and his chest, and some spots of blood were at the top of the stairs. I do not think, members of the jury, that you need pay much attention to those spots, because they were probably caused by

Stephen's choking, as he would do while he remained conscious. The hands of the dead man were found to be quite clean.

At 7.30 am Detective Inspector Winter was called. He found that the revolver was five-chambered; there were five cartridges in it, two of which had been fired, but in the revolving chamber they were not in immediate sequence. They ran in this order: Discharged, live, discharged, live, live.

Inspector Winter saw Mrs Barney in the lounge. When he asked her: 'Can you tell me about this tragedy?' she lost her temper, began to shout, and ordered him out of the house. He tried to reason with her, and eventually she became calmer. He asked to whom the revolver belonged, and she said it was hers. The officer said: 'I want some explanation of the shooting. He has undoubtedly been shot.' She again flew into a temper and ordered him out of the house. She said: 'Let me go upstairs to him. I want him.'

She calmed down again and asked for a dress. She was wearing some kind of a gown at the time. A dress was brought down and the inspector asked again about the revolver. She said: 'It is mine. I have had it a long time. Last night we had a quarrel. He got the revolver from a chair. We struggled and it went off. It is terrible. Leave me alone.'

She put on the dress, and directly afterwards the telephone rang. She tried to get at it, but the police officer would not allow her to do so. He answered it, and this brought down further abuse on the police officers. It was repeated with great frequency during the time they were there.

The inspector told her he wanted to take her to Gerald Road Police Station to obtain a statement, and asked her to put on a hat and coat which were in the room. She preferred a hat and coat upstairs. Inspector Campion suggested that the coat downstairs would probably be a better garment as it was fur and she might find the police station rather cold. At this she flew into a paroxysm of rage and rushed across to Inspector Campion and struck him a violent blow on the face, saying: 'I will teach you to say you will put me in a

o Appear at the Gaiety : A Society Girl Stage Recruit.

TO ACT IN " THE BLUE KITTEN " : MISS DOLORES MULLENS (MISS DOLORES ASHLEY).

Miss Elvira Dolores Mullens is the elder daughter of Sir John and Lady Mullens, and is the sister of Princess George Imeretinsky. She went on the stage a year ago. She is to appear in " The Blue Kitten," the forthcoming production at the Gaiety, in which Miss Ethel Levey and Mr. W. H. Berry will be seen, which is promised for Dec. 23. Her stage name is Dolores Ashley.

PHOTOGRAPHS BY LENARE, EXCLUSIVE TO " THE SKETCH."

(left) Body being removed from 21 Williams Mews *(Radio Times Hulton Picture Library)*

(right) 21 Williams Mews as it is today *(Pipe-Rich)*

cell, you vile swine.' This is told to you so that you may see what sort of temper this woman gives way to on slight provocation. She had to be restrained. One did not quite know what she was going to do next.

The telephone rang again and was again answered by the inspector, who realised it was Lady Mullens speaking and said to her: 'If you are Lady Mullens, you must come round to the house for any information you desire.'

As soon as the inspector mentioned Lady Mullens's name, Mrs Barney forced her way to the telephone and spoke through it. After she had put down the receiver, she said: 'Now you know who my mother is perhaps you will be a little more careful what you say and do. I will teach you to say you will take me to a police station.'

Within five minutes her father and mother arrived, and at 9.30 they and the inspector went to the police station with Mrs Barney, who, after being cautioned, made the following statement:

I am twenty-seven years of age . . . and have been residing at Williams Mews for about a year. I am a married woman living apart from my husband who is at present in America. The last I heard of him he was a singer. He left me about two-and-a-half years ago . . . I have known a man named Michael Scott Stephen for about a year. I was introduced to him through friends.

We were great friends and he used to come and see me from time to time. He had no occupation. He always used to see me home and last night he did so as usual. We arrived home at 2 am. Immediately we got in we had a quarrel about a woman he was fond of. He knew I had a revolver in the house. I have had it for years. I do not know where it came from. It was kept in various places. Last night it was under the cushion of a chair in the bedroom, near the bed. I was afraid of it and I used to hide it from time to time. He knew where it was last night. He took it from under the chair saying, 'I am going to take it away for fear you will kill yourself.' He went into the room on the left. I ran after him and tried to get it back. There was no struggle in the bedroom. He was outside in the spare room in the doorway. As we were struggling together—he wanted to take it away and I wanted

D

to get it back—it went off. Our hands were together, his hands in mine . . .

SIR PATRICK HASTINGS *asked that* SIR PERCIVAL *should read from the original statement.*

SIR PERCIVAL CLARKE: 'Our hands were together, his hands in mine, for a few minutes. I did not think anything had happened.'

MR JUSTICE HUMPHREYS: Is there a full stop after 'his hands in mine'?

SIR PERCIVAL CLARKE: No, there is a comma.

MR JUSTICE HUMPHREYS: As I understand it, that is the end of the sentence.

SIR PERCIVAL CLARKE: I do not want to put a wrong interpretation upon it and we had better ask the officer. (*He continued to read the statement.*)

I did not think anything had happened. It seemed quite all right.

I did not think anything serious. He went into the bathroom and half shut the door. He said, 'Fetch a doctor.' I asked, 'Do you really mean it?' I did not have the revolver then. I think it had fallen to the ground.

I saw he looked ill, I rang up the doctor and no one answered. I went upstairs and saw him sitting on the floor. I was upset and began to cry. I again rang up the doctor and he said he would come. I went upstairs again. Stephen said, 'Why does not the doctor come? I want to tell him what has happened. It was not your fault.' He repeated that over and over again. I tried to cut his tie off. I put a towel on his chest and got pillows. I again rang up the doctor and they said he was leaving. I again went upstairs and saw he was dead and just waited. I don't remember what I did afterwards, I was so frantic. I am sure, as far as I know, there was only one shot fired.

Stephen and I have quarrelled on previous occasions, but not often.

Inspector Winter went back to 21 Williams Mews. He found the telephone extension, and near it, attached to the wall, was a piece of paper; written on this was 'Police, SLO 5106'. That was the number of the police at Gerald Road.

There appeared to be no sign of a struggle anywhere. The police found two letters—one typewritten from Mrs Barney to Michael, and another from Michael to her. Later they found in the bathroom a box containing ten cartridges, nine of which were live and one spent. Photographs were taken, and Mrs Barney was allowed to go to her parents' house.

SIR PERCIVAL *indicated, by pointing to his left breast, the position of the fatal wound.*

There appeared to be some blackening on the upper edge of the pullover above the lapel, and there was blackening or scorching of the hands or wrists, sleeves or cuffs of the jacket or shirt.

Sir Bernard Spilsbury, the pathologist, will say that the direction of the wound was directly and horizontally from front to back, and that the bullet was found embedded near the rib corresponding at the back to the point of entry. Sir Bernard will also say that a person so wounded would be likely to remain conscious for a short while, then collapse into unconsciousness and die within ten minutes. The blood which had escaped indicated that during the conscious interval, while he was bleeding, the man was in a sitting or standing position.

The revolver is one of the safest made, for it is hammerless and the trigger admits but one finger. The hammer cannot be cocked by hand, and the pull to secure the firing of the pistol is a long and heavy one, for not only has it to raise the internal main spring, but it has also to revolve the chambers. The revolver weighs 13oz, but the pull is 14lb, and it requires that you should hold it firmly to discharge it at all. The cylinder rotates as it is fired, and there is a little space between the cylinder and the middle end of the barrel; through that, on the revolver being fired, there is an escape of gas which would carry with it smoke or a discharge of a black colour.

You will hear that the medical evidence can definitely establish the direction in which the revolver was held when fired, and you can estimate very fairly the distance from the coat at which the muzzle of the pistol was when it was fired. You will be told it was not less than three inches and not more than six inches away. You will see from this that, to all intents and purposes, it is practically impossible that Michael Stephen could have caused this injury to himself.

Someone pressed the trigger. That is necessary, for the revolver will not go off without, and if he did not, who did? There was only one other person besides Michael Stephen at that place, and when the charge was made against Mrs Barney —she was arrested on the charge of murdering Michael Stephen—she said: 'I did not shoot him. I am not guilty.'

If she did not shoot him, who did? If she did, then it becomes material for you to consider whether she did it by accident or design. You will bear in mind her own admission of the quarrel which had started when they got back.

You will not lose the significance of the cause of the quarrel which she alleges existed, and you will not lose sight of the fact that there was that warning shout before the pistol was fired, in her voice: 'Get out, get out, I will shoot you. I will shoot you.' Then the pistol was fired.

It was not the first time there had been a quarrel. You will hear that there was often quarrelling, but if the defence be raised that this was entirely an accident it becomes very material, in my submission, for you to consider any evidence which can be laid before you as to whether it was an accident or intentional.

About 3 am on 19 May there was a terrible row between Mrs Barney and Stephen. It started, I think, over a taxi-man. She was in a state of hysteria. That row was followed by her screaming out of a first-floor window, telling Stephen to go away. You will hear he was asking for money, and she told him to go away. Later he returned and rang the bell, but he was seen to walk away again. You will hear how far he went before Mrs Barney, looking out of the window, shouted: 'Laugh, baby; laugh for the last time.' She was observed holding something bright in her hand. There was a flash, smoke, and the loud report of a pistol. Stephen was not hit. You will hear how he went away and spent the night in a greengrocer's van at the end of the mews. That was not the only quarrel.

Every unlawful killing is presumed to be murder unless it is proved otherwise. You will look with anxiety and care to see if the death of this young man is explained, not by any vague, confused suggestion of accident in the course of a struggle, but by any evidence consistent with common sense which will enable you to understand how this young man came to his death unless she deliberately fired the pistol.

Before the evidence for the Prosecution was called, SIR PATRICK HASTINGS *asked that all the witnesses, except the police, should remain out of court.*

MR JUSTICE HUMPHREYS: Including Sir Bernard Spilsbury?

SIR PATRICK HASTINGS: I do not press that, but I should prefer everyone excepting the police to be out of court.

MR JUSTICE HUMPHREYS: You are entitled to have everybody out of court if you wish it. Be it so.

EVIDENCE FOR THE PROSECUTION

DETECTIVE SERGEANT ALBERT MADDEN *of Scotland Yard gave evidence of the taking of a number of photographs of the interior of 21 Williams Mews and of the position of the deceased's body.*

Cross-examined by SIR PATRICK HASTINGS, *the witness said that, so far as he knew, nothing in the room was moved up to the time he took the photographs. To the best of his belief, the photographs gave a correct representation of the various rooms at the time Mr Stephen died.*

FRANCIS RICHARD STEPHEN, *a solicitor and a brother of the deceased, of Glendarvon Street, Putney, SW, said the dead man's last occupation was that of a dress designer. So far as he knew, his brother had not done any work recently.*

Cross-examined by SIR PATRICK HASTINGS:

Did you say at the inquest that your brother was formerly supported by your father?—Yes.

Your father stopped it about three years ago?—Yes.

Did you say that your mother let your brother have money when he was in difficulties?—Yes.

And that you did yourself?—Yes.

But that you stopped advancing him money some nine months ago, having got tired of it?—That is so.

Your brother, so far as was known, had no means of

supporting himself?—I understand that as recently as a month before his death he had financial support of £30 or £40 from his mother.

Your brother was very good-looking?—I think people might have regarded him as such.

In reply to SIR PERCIVAL CLARKE, *re-examining, the witness said he did not know of any earnings the dead man had made during the last four or five months of his life.*

How was he living?—I don't know.

Was he a weak or a strong man?—Physically I think he was fairly strong, but his actual health was not strong.

Would it be right to say that he was a man of small bones – wrists, hands and feet?—No.

HUGH ARMIGEL WADE, *a composer, gave evidence that he had known Stephen for about three years, but knew Mrs Barney better than he had known Stephen.*

Were you one of the cocktail party?—I was.

How many more were there?—About 29 or 30.

Who served the cocktails?—Mr Stephen.

How long were you there?—About an hour, from 6.30 to 7.30.

Did you go to the Blue Angel Club?—I did.

Did you see Mrs Barney and Stephen?—About 11.30 at the club.

On what terms did they appear to be?—I did not see them together.

What was the last time you saw either of them that night? —Between 11.30 and 12.

ARTHUR TILDEN JEFFRESS of *Orchard Court, Portland Square, stated that he was of independent means. He had known Mrs Barney for four or five years, and knew Stephen slightly.*

MR BYRNE (*for the Crown*): Did you see him on the night of 30 May?—Yes. At a cocktail party at Mrs Barney's flat.

What time did you arrive there?—About a quarter to eight.

What time did you leave?—At ten o'clock.

Were there any remaining there?—There were no others.

Did you leave Stephen behind?—No, the three of us left together.

Did you have dinner with them later that evening?—Yes, at the Café de Paris.

And after dinner did you go with them to the Blue Angel Club?—Yes.

What time did they leave that club?—Between half-past twelve and a quarter to one.

You did not go with them?—No.

Upon what terms were they that evening?—Friendly.

MRS DOROTHY HALL, *wife of a chauffeur of 10 Williams Mews (nearly opposite No 21) said she knew Mrs Barney, and first saw Stephen go to her flat as a visitor about August last.*

Had he been a frequent visitor to No 21?—Yes.

At any time of the day or night?—Any time.

The witness said that at 4 am on 31 May she heard people rowing, the voices coming from No 21. She heard a woman screaming.

Did you know the voice sufficiently well to tell me who it was?—Mrs Barney. One of the windows of Mrs Barney's flat was open. I did not hear enough to hear what the row was about, but I heard Mr Stephen's voice raised. I looked out of my window and heard Mrs Barney say that she was going to shoot. She said it twice.

Did you hear anything before she said that she would shoot?—No, just the screaming and rowing.

When you heard her say that, did you hear any answer?—I heard a shot.

Where did the shot appear to come from?—From their front room. I heard Mr Stephen shout: 'What have you done?' Mrs Barney was screaming out: 'Chicken, come back to me; I will do anything I can for you.' Mrs Barney was crying and very hysterical. She 'phoned the doctor that someone had shot himself. The doctor arrived shortly afterwards.

Was that the first time you heard sounds of firearms from that place?—About three weeks previously there was shooting. Mrs Barney fired out of the window.

MR JUSTICE HUMPHREYS: You mean you saw Mrs Barney fire?—Yes.

SIR PERCIVAL CLARKE: What time was that?—In the early hours of the morning.

What attracted your attention?—It was a row between a taxi-man and Mrs Barney. He was going on about damage done to his cab, and Mrs Barney was saying she was very sorry. Mrs Barney went indoors and the taxi went away.

What attracted your attention next?—Mrs Barney screaming out of the window to Mr Stephen and telling him to clear away before she sent for the police.

Where was Mr Stephen?—He was at her door talking and calling and asking her for money.

Did she give him any?—She told him to go and fish for it. Mr Stephen went away in the taxi-cab in which he had arrived and then returned, walking. I saw Mr Stephen going away from the house and Mrs Barney looked out of the window and said: 'Laugh, baby; laugh for the last time,' and she fired.

How was she dressed?—I don't think she had anything on.

How do you know she fired?—I saw her and heard the shot.

Did you see in which hand she held the pistol?—The left.

Where was Mr Stephen standing?—Practically outside my door.

Did he appear to be hit?—No. He told Mrs Barney not to be so foolish as everybody was looking at them.

Did she go inside?—She fell as though she had fainted.

Where did Michael go?—He got into a greengrocer's van standing in the mews.

Had you heard quarrelling between them before?—Many times.

SIR PATRICK HASTINGS: About eleven o'clock that morning, some hours after you had seen Stephen get into a greengrocer's van, did you see him and Mrs Barney leave the flat together?—Yes.

Did they seem to be on the best possible terms?—Very friendly.

SIR PATRICK HASTINGS *proceeded to cross-examine the wit-*

ness with regard to evidence she gave at the police court that she spoke to Mr Stephen from her window:

In the police court, there the matter ended. Now I want to ask you to be very, very careful in your answer and tell us what did Stephen say to you?

SIR PERCIVAL CLARKE *objected to the question:*

The Prosecution at the police court considered that what was said to Mr Stephen not in the presence of the prisoner could not be evidence, and therefore it was not tendered. As it was not evidence for the Crown, it could not be admissible as evidence for the Defence.

SIR PATRICK HASTINGS *replied that in his experience at the Bar such a thing had never been stated before. That the Prosecution should have asked a question in the lower court and then not allowed it to be answered was, he submitted, most unfair to the Defence.*

In these days we all know what the result of such a question being asked and left unanswered is. Here the Prosecution proved a fact. They have proved there was the firing of a revolver from a window and that the deceased man at the moment made a statement to a witness. I submit it is always admissible to give evidence of a statement accompanying such an incident.

SIR PATRICK *recalled that at the time of the Lord George Gordon riots the observations of the mob were admitted as evidence.*

MR JUSTICE HUMPHREYS *observed that he was of opinion that the objection was properly taken and the matter was not free from doubt, but in this case he would not exclude it.*

SIR PATRICK HASTINGS: You said at the police court that immediately after the shot was fired the deceased spoke to you at the window. What did he say?—He apologised for being such a nuisance in the mews. I told him to clear off as he was a perfect nuisance. He said he was afraid to leave Mrs Barney for fear she would commit suicide.

Did I rightly understand you to say that when the shot was fired you saw a puff of smoke?—Yes.

Was it a big puff of smoke?—(*The witness extended her arms to describe it.*) Well, not very big, just ordinary.

You don't know that cordite cartridges don't make any smoke at all?—No.

Do you happen to know that the name by which Mrs Barney frequently addressed Stephen was Mickey?—It might have been.

Are you prepared to pledge your oath that the words she used were not 'Mickey, Mickey, don't leave me'?—I am quite sure the word she used was 'Chicken'.

If you are wrong about that, and the word was 'Mickey', do you think you are as likely to be wrong about anything else you heard?—I still say the word she used was 'Chicken'.

Later the witness agreed that the words used were 'Chicken, chicken, come back to me', and not, 'Chicken, chicken, don't leave me'.

MRS KATE STEVENS, *wife of John Leslie Stevens, a chauffeur, of 8 Williams Mews, said she saw people arriving for the cocktail party*:

During that time Mr Stephen went out with another lady. He walked out of the mews, and soon afterwards Mrs Barney and another man went out in a motor. I saw Mr Stephen come back in a taxi-cab with a lady. It was, I think, a few minutes afterwards that I saw Mrs Barney come back with a gentleman. She had some siphons of soda-water in her hand, and when she got out of the car she seemed to have a few words with the gentleman. Then she went into the house, and I did not see Mrs Barney any more until she came to the door to say good-bye to the gentleman. I went to bed about 11.30 and I did not hear anything until my dog woke me up. He was barking and I got up and told him to be quiet. Then I heard two shots fired. I went to the window but I could see no one. I got back again into bed, and I heard two more shots. I said to my husband: 'That is Mrs Barney firing a pistol.'

Did you see anyone?—No. I went to bed again, and then I heard a final shot, which was very much louder than the others.

Where did the loud one come from?—It seemed to me from the bedroom.

Did you hear voices?—I heard Mrs Barney and a man quarrelling, but I did not recognise the voice.

Did you hear any words?—Not until after the loud shot. It sounded to me as if Mr Stephen said: 'What made you do it?' Mrs Barney said: 'Michael, Michael, come back. I love you,' and she kept repeating it.

Further questioned, the witness said that on two previous occasions she had heard shots in the mews. The first time was about five weeks before 31 May, when the sound of a shot, not very loud, came from No 21. About a fortnight before 31 May, Mrs Barney fired at Mr Stephen, saying: 'Smile, baby, smile for the last time'.

SIR PATRICK HASTINGS: Do you know that the story you are telling today is very different from what you told the magistrate?—No. I didn't tell the magistrate everything because he did not ask me.

There was a regular fusillade going on in the mews?—There must have been.

You have heard many shots?—I think many people have heard them, but I think they are not public-spirited enough to come forward.

MR JUSTICE HUMPHREYS: Have you ever heard a pistol fired?—Yes, when somebody was cleaning one.

Do you think that the sounds you heard were pistol shots and not something else?—I am quite sure they were pistol shots, although they were not so loud as the two fired on the 31st.

WILLIAM KIFF, *a chauffeur living next door to Mrs Barney, said that he was awakened about 4 am on 31 May by hearing Mrs Barney screaming. At 4.35 am he heard a revolver fired; the noise came from upstairs in Mrs Barney's flat. He dressed and went into the mews.*

I believe you made a noise there yourself?—Yes, I threw a piece of gas-iron at the cat; it struck the air vent of a manhole, and possibly hit the dustbin.

DR THOMAS DURRANT, *of Westbourne Terrace, Paddington, said that he had known Mrs Barney for six years, and had*

*attended her professionally. At about 4.30 am on 31 May the
telephone bell rang, and his wife, who answered it, did not
get in touch with the person ringing:*

The telephone rang again three or four minutes later, and
I answered it. Mrs Barney was speaking.

What passed over the telephone?—There was a flood of
incoherency. She was hysterical, crying: 'Come at once, come
at once. Jump into a taxi – it has happened here.' She said
that a gentleman had shot himself. Before I was dressed the
telephone rang again, and again Mrs Barney was on the telephone. She was reproachful. 'Why haven't you come? – why
haven't you come? Come at once. Jump into a taxi. He is
bleeding,' she kept saying. Mrs Barney let me into her flat.
She was very overwrought, very excited, very hysterical. She
kept saying: 'Why didn't you come before? Why didn't you
come?' in a most reproachful way. I said: 'I have come as
soon as I possibly can. What is the matter?' There was a
certain amount of incoherency, but as far as I recollect she
said: 'Come and see, come and see.' I went upstairs and she
followed behind. When I reached the bend of the stairs I
saw the body of a man lying at the top of the stairs.

Was Mrs Barney there while you were examining him?—
Yes. She was about three stairs below me. She was talking. I
might almost call it babbling. She said: 'Is he dead? – he
can't be dead. I love him so. Can you do anything for him?
He wanted to see you and tell you it was an accident.'

Did she touch the dead man at all?—Not at that time, but
shortly afterwards. I said: 'If you go into the bedroom I will
tell you how he is.' As she left the position she was in, she
leaned forward and kissed him and then passed in front of
me into the bedroom. I followed. I put my foot over the
revolver.

Did you do that in consequence of anything she said?—
Yes, she said: 'Let me die, let me die. I will kill myself.' I
told Mrs Barney to pull herself together as I would have to
send for the police. She replied: 'Don't do that, my mother
must not know. She is ill, it will kill her.'

Were you able to control her?—With great difficulty. She
was catching hold of me by the sleeve and shoulders and

almost screaming. It was a very painful scene altogether. When I demanded an explanation of what had happened, Mrs Barney said that she and Stephen had quarrelled at a party the previous evening on the question of some woman she thought he was consorting with. They had gone out later and dined with a friend, gone to a club, and returned in the small hours of the morning and had gone to bed. She said they had been wrangling again about the woman. Further to that, Mrs Barney said that Stephen eventually got very angry, and said that he would get up and go to this other woman. He had got up and began dressing. She had said: 'If you go away, you know what I will do,' and indicated to him an easy chair situated at the side of the bed. Mrs Barney told me that Stephen knew the revolver was under the cushion of the chair, that he went to the chair, picked up the revolver, and started to go out of the room with it in his hand. She followed him out of the room and they began wrestling in the passage-way. She was trying to get the gun from his hand, and they were wrestling together when the revolver went off, she did not know how. She did not think there was any hurt done, but he looked up in surprise and went into the bathroom, partly closing the door behind him. She called out to him: 'Come back to me, Michael, come back to me,' and he said: 'Call the doctor. Call the doctor.' Eventually he opened the door and came outside. He looked very ill. He was holding his side with his hand. She then went downstairs and apparently made the first ring on the telephone. That was about 4.40 or 4.45. May I say that I have put it into my own words as I best remember what she told me. The general sense is as I have described it, but her words were in broken pieces, and I have fitted them together. I have said all the things she told me as far as I can remember.

Did she say anything about the attitude of her mind when he said he was going to leave her?—Yes, that she was so angry that she would commit suicide, and he said: 'Well, at all events, you won't do it with this.'

Did she mention anything about a quarrel she had had with Michael?—Yes. She said that she had often quarrelled with him and that sometimes he had treated her very badly and that she was terrified of him at times; that she had had to call for assistance on occasions to have him removed and that he had broken the kitchen window in his attempts to get in. She spoke about intending to commit suicide if he left her.

MR JUSTICE HUMPHREYS: Did you understand when she said that she had threatened to commit suicide that it was to him she had made the threats?—That is what I gathered.

Cross-examined by SIR PATRICK HASTINGS:

You have told us how she appeared. You were the first person to see Mrs Barney after this occurrence. I want to hear a little more of what she said. Did she appear to be passionately devoted to this dead man?—Oh, yes.

Did she kiss him after he was dead?—Yes, several times.

And did her actions appear to you, so far as you could judge, to be absolutely sincere and genuine?—Certainly.

In your opinion, was she in a mental condition when you saw her that she could possibly have invented a story that was not true?—Certainly not. She was in such a crazy state of mind that I could not see how anyone could, with such disjointed sentences, collect them together and make a collective history of the case.

Whether you are right or wrong, had you the slightest doubt in your mind that she was telling you what she thought, telling you anything other than what she thought was true? —No.

Has anything happened to make you alter your opinion since?—No.

I just want one test. She spoke of her mother being ill. Is Lady Mullens ill?—She was very ill and overwrought, as would be natural after such a strain.

Yes, but before that, had she been suffering from her heart?—She has suffered from her heart.

Now there is one question of fact. I am not sure what you did with your foot so far as the revolver is concerned. Did you put your foot on the revolver?—I never touched it.

The witness, taking his spectacles to represent the revolver and the Testament to represent his foot, demonstrated how he held his foot over the revolver to shield it without touching it.

Is it a common occurrence for a man to be shot in the upper part of the lung and live?—There is no reason why he should not.

Speaking as a medical man, after seeing the post-mortem examination, are you able to tell me how long he lived after he was shot?—I should not have expected him to have died very quickly if I had simply examined the wound through the lung. I should possibly have expected him to live some hours.

In your view, is it humanly possible to give a period of time in minutes to that man's life?—I should not like to. I doubt that Stephen died within ten minutes. The dripping of blood showed that he had stood up after he was shot.

PC WILLIAM ANDREWS *of 'C' Division said that when he was called to Mrs Barney's flat at 5.35 am on 31 May, Mrs Barney said: 'I called the doctor and did my best for him.'*

DR ARNOLD HARPER, *police divisional surgeon, said he considered that Mr Stephen had been dead one or two hours when he arrived at the flat at 6.30 am.*

Did you notice whether the hands were stained or dirty?— They were clean.

Before the Court rose, SIR PATRICK HASTINGS *asked that Sir John and Lady Mullens should be granted permission to see their daughter Mrs Barney, for a few minutes before she went back to prison.*

MR JUSTICE HUMPHREYS: I have no objection.

SECOND DAY   *Tuesday, 5 July*

DETECTIVE INSPECTOR WILLIAM WINTER *of 'C' Division, examined by* MR BYRNE, *stated that he went to Mrs Barney's flat at 7.30 am on 31 May and saw the body of Michael Stephen. A revolver was near the outside of the left wrist. In the lounge he saw Mrs Barney:*

She was wearing a kind of kimono. The revolver had five chambers which contained two discharged and three live cartridges. I examined the bedroom and found that it was not unduly disturbed. The bed gave one the impression that it had been occupied by two persons. The floor of the spare room was covered with polished linoleum.

Were there any marks on the linoleum?—There were none. I went down to the kitchenette, where I found 30 glasses on the table, four empty siphons, and a cocktail-shaker. Under the sink were five empty bottles, two of which had contained vermouth and three gin. I went into the lounge and saw Mrs Barney, who told me her name and age and said that Stephen was a friend of hers. When I asked how the tragedy had happened she began to shout and ordered me out of the house. I reasoned with her, and she eventually calmed down. She told me that the revolver was hers. When I told her I wanted some explanation about Stephen, she flew into a temper and again ordered me out of the house, shouting: 'Let me go upstairs to him. I want him.' Mrs Barney asked for a dress to put on, and it was brought to her. When she had put it on she said that the revolver was hers, and went on: 'Last night we had a quarrel. He got the revolver from the chair. We struggled and it went off. It is terrible. Leave me alone.' She was asked to go to the police station to make a statement, and Inspector Campion, who was with me, suggested that she should put on a fur coat which was in the room. At that Mrs Barney flew into a temper, went over to where Inspector Campion was standing, and struck him a heavy blow on the side of his face. She said: 'I'll teach you to tell me you will put me in a cell, you foul swine!'

As the result of her demeanour, what did you have to do? —I had to restrain her. I had to hold her away from Inspector Campion. Before we left for the police station the telephone bell rang and I found that it was Lady Mullens speaking. Mrs Barney rushed to the telephone and shouted down it: 'Mummy, Mummy!' Then she turned to the police officers and said: 'Now you know who my mother is, you will be more careful in what you do and say to me. I will teach you to say that you will take me to a police station.' Mrs Barney's

The Judge: Mr Justice Humphreys

(below left) For the Crown: Sir Percival Clarke *(Radio Times Hulton Picture Library)*

(below right) For the Defence: Sir Patrick Hastings *(Keystone Press)*

Police holding back crowds during the trial *(Radio Times Hulton Picture Library)*

Mrs Barney – a free woman – leaves her car the next day *(Radio Times Hulton Picture Library)*

father and mother came to the flat, and we all went to the police station, where Mrs Barney made a statement.

I later returned to the flat and made a further examination. During the course of it, I found two letters.

CLERK OF THE COURT *read the letters. The first, written on mauve notepaper, was from the dead man to Mrs Barney. The notepaper was headed '21 Williams Mews', but this had been struck out and the words 'Love Hut' written above it. It was in the following terms*:

Baby, Little Capable,
This little note is to be awaiting your arrival in the place in which I have been happiest all my life. Be brave, my dear, dear darling, and take care of yourself for me, because you're mine.
Don't forget your Mickums (you came downstairs here, honey, so I had to hide this under my coat so as you would not see it; hence the smudges).
Forgive me all the dreadful horrible things I have done, baby. I promise to be better and kinder so that you won't be frightened any more.
I love you, only you, in all the world.

MICKESH

SIR PATRICK HASTINGS *asked that the last sentence should be repeated and the* CLERK OF THE COURT *did so.*

SIR PATRICK HASTINGS: I think the signature is probably 'Mickey'.

CLERK OF THE COURT: There is a postscript: 'You've just called, "What are you doing?" so must stop.'

The second letter reads:

21 William Mews,
Lowndes Square, S.W.
Sloane 6860

Tuesday evening

My darling baby,
I nearly had heart failure reading your letter, it was so divine. I have never been so thrilled over reading anything before.
I am sorry to reply on the typewriter, but I am rushing it

E

rather so that I can post it early and you might get it in the morning, darling, long before I arrive down.

I am terrified you might not get the letter, so I won't say much, but I really do love you, darling, and even if this note was lost I would not care if anyone knew how much I love you.

You hand me the biggest thrills I have ever had, my sweet, and all I hope is we can go on being thrilled endlessly. I adore it when you are sweet and kind to me, as I have not had a lot of affection in my life as you have had.

So you see it means a great deal and I feel like suicide when you are angry.

Sometimes when you are feeling furious do try to think of the hell I had to endure with J. B. and then you will relent, I think. Don't be too jealous with me either, Baby, please as I suffered so much from that with him and if you trust me you won't need to be jealous. It absolutely ruined my marriage before and it leads to all kinds of misery, so do be a bit broadminded.

I won't let you down. God knows why I should when you are so lovely. I do hope you will be well soon, my darling. Take care of yourself for me. All my love, really all,

ELVIRA

I will read your letter dozens of times when I am in bed to-night. I could not wait until then to read it but I was alone as I promised and I drank to you, darling.

THE WITNESS: When Mrs Barney was charged on 3 June she said: 'I did not shoot him. I am not guilty.'

Cross-examined by SIR PATRICK HASTINGS:

Mrs Barney spoke of her great unhappiness with someone who was identified as 'J.B.'?—Yes.

Are 'J.B.' the initials of her husband?—Yes.

As the result of your inquiries, are you aware that Mrs Barney had communicated with the police station to ask for help on previous occasions?—Yes.

You have no doubt that Mrs Barney was terribly distraught? —Oh, yes, she was.

After striking Inspector Campion, did she apologise to him for having hit him?—She apologised to me for doing it.

As the result of your inquiries, can you tell me whether anyone complained to the police about an attempted murder in the mews about a fortnight previously?—I have been unable to trace a report of such an occurrence from anybody.

Or a report of any shooting?—Yes.

No complaint of any sort or kind?—Not to the police.

Have the police made any efforts to find whether, in the mews, there is the slightest mark of a bullet having been fired into it?—Yes. A very thorough examination of the mews has been made.

Is there any trace of a bullet having been fired into it?— Not that one could say with any certainty at all.

In the police court you said: 'No traces of any kind were found'?—That is so, Sir.

If anyone took up this revolver, you would expect to find fingerprints on it afterwards?—Yes.

But, if two people struggled, it would be likely that the fingerprints would be undecipherable?—That is so.

Was this revolver examined for fingerprints?—Yes.

Was it found that the marks on it were so blurred that no fingerprints were decipherable except one?—That is so.

Whose was that one?—That was mine.

You had picked it up with the greatest care?—Yes. The fingerprints both of the dead man and of Mrs Barney had been taken. Mrs Barney was very distraught, but all the statements she made to the police were to the same effect.

Can you tell me whether, if a soft lead bullet hit a wall, you would not expect to find a 'splash of lead' on the wall? —Yes, I would.

These were soft lead bullets?—Yes.

Re-examined by SIR PERCIVAL CLARKE:

With regard to Mrs Barney's previous communications with the police, who do you mean?—She has rung up and asked for police to go round to her place to eject people.

Have those requests been responded to?—Some.

Did any request relate to Michael Stephen?—Not so far as I am aware.

DETECTIVE INSPECTOR EDWARD CAMPION *of 'C' Division con-*

firmed the previous witness's evidence as to the defendant's demeanour before she was taken to the police station.

Cross-examined, he said that, before she left, she asked to be allowed to see Stephen's body again.

SIR PATRICK HASTINGS: Was she allowed to?—No, Sir.

Why not?—I cannot tell you. Perhaps it was not thought advisable.

Have any steps been taken to see whether Mrs Barney has handled the cartridge box within the last six months?—No, Sir.

SIR BERNARD SPILSBURY, *Honorary Pathologist to the Home Office*:

I went to Mrs Barney's flat at about 1.30 pm on 31 May and saw Stephen's dead body. The man had been dead for a number of hours. There was a hole in the dead man's coat and some marks round it. I have seen similar marks in other cases which had been caused by smoke, but they might also be dust marks. The hands and wrists were perfectly clean. There was no smoke on them, nor any scorching or singeing; nor were there any smoke marks, scorching or singeing on the shirt-sleeves or the coat sleeves.

At the post-mortem examination I formed the opinion from the way in which blood had run down the body, that the deceased had been either standing or in a sitting position for some time after he had received the injury, until, probably, he collapsed in an unconscious condition.

Stephen was 5ft 8½in in height and was muscular. The wound was 2¾in below the left collar bone and 3in to the left of the middle line of the front of the body. It was horizontal from back to front. Assuming that Stephen was standing when the wound was inflicted, it would be 4ft 5in high from the ground. The bullet went straight across the left chest, neither up nor down, and struck the top of the sixth rib, where it remained.

I made a test with a skeleton used in teaching medical students, and this confirmed that the course of the bullet was horizontal. The lung wound would produce a rapid flow of blood. That flow of blood would produce unconsciousness within a short period, and death, in my view, not more than ten minutes after the injury was inflicted.

SIR PERCIVAL CLARKE: Did it enter into your mind when inquiring into the cause of death to consider the possibility of suicide?—That, of course, was one of the possibilities I had to take into account. Such a possibility did not appear to be a reasonable one. In the first place, the bullet had not been fired from close to the body in the sense of touching it, at any rate as is usual in suicide injuries; it was also unlike suicides in that the aim was at the chest instead of the heart. The weapon requires both a long and heavy pull. The trigger has to be moved right back before it can be let off.

MR JUSTICE HUMPHREYS: The jury will be given an opportunity to test the revolver for themselves.

THE WITNESS (*pointing the revolver towards his heart*): I find it impossible to discharge it holding it in this position, about three inches from the body. With the wrist bent as it must be bent I could not get enough power to discharge the pistol off at all.

Cross-examined by SIR PATRICK HASTINGS:

In order to qualify yourself to give evidence here today, to show that this bullet was fired in a perfectly horizontal position, I gather you had to examine the skeleton of someone else?—Well, I had to confirm it upon the skeleton of someone else.

Is it a natural proposition that in every human body there is a difference, more or less, in the formation of that body?— Yes, in the formation of the bones.

And the best way to see whether a bullet is fired straight into the body is to look at the actual body?—Yes.

MR JUSTICE HUMPHREYS: And did you look at it?—I did, My Lord, and I formed the opinion that it was horizontal, and not only by looking at it but by measuring it.

SIR PATRICK HASTINGS: No further questions, My Lord.

ROBERT CHURCHILL, *gun-maker, of 39–42 Leicester Square*: I have had a lifelong experience of firearms and shooting. I examined the revolver on 6 June. It was an American weapon, made by Smith & Wesson; five-chambered and of

·32 calibre. There was no external hammer. It had evidently been fired recently and was in good working order. The weapon weighed just under 13 ounces and had a 14lb pull. When the trigger was pulled, the cylinder rotated. Anyone, by placing a finger on the cylinder, could prevent the weapon from being fired.

SIR PERCIVAL CLARKE: Supposing any person was holding it by the cylinder?—I can grip the cylinder and prevent anyone else firing it.

Can anybody else do that? Does it require a strong grip?—No. One finger can stop it.

Is it in your view a dangerous or safe weapon?—It is always considered to be one of the safest revolvers made.

How far away from the clothes was the muzzle of the revolver, in your opinion, when fired?—Not absolutely touching or within an inch. I estimated it at a distance of three inches.

Supposing it was first of all fired in the mews, would you expect to find any trace of the ammunition left after a fortnight?—The bullet would be smashed against a stone or other hard substance, and I should not expect to find it.

Cross-examined by SIR PATRICK HASTINGS:

(*Holding the revolver.*) Do you seriously say that this is one of the safest weapons made?—Yes.

In most good hammerless revolvers is there not a safety device to render them more safe, while this has no safety device?—That is so. I meant that it is safer than a revolver with a hammer or an automatic pistol.

It does not require any terrific muscular development to fire it?—It would require more pulling if the weapon were held loosely. The weapon has a 14lb pull.

MR JUSTICE HUMPHREYS: What is the meaning of a 14lb pull?—The dead weight required to pull the trigger.

SIR PATRICK, *in illustrating the ease with which he was able to pull the trigger of the revolver, pointed it towards a barrister who sat in the seats behind him; the barrister moved his head to one side.*

SIR PATRICK HASTINGS: It is perfectly safe. (*To the witness*) Almost invariably, is not the tendency of a person who is not skilled with a revolver to throw it up?—Unless they flinch and pull it down.

You know, do you not, that there were in this revolver when it was found one cartridge which had been exploded, then a live cartridge, and then an exploded cartridge?—Quite.

Have you noticed anything peculiar about this revolver if you half-pull the trigger?—If you half-pull, the first pull or pressure rotates the cylinder.

Supposing circumstances in which that revolver went through the stage of this trigger being half-pulled and the finger pressed two or three times, do you notice what happens? (SIR PATRICK *illustrated how the cylinder rotated.*) So that when you finally get a complete pull, one cartridge has gone right past the barrel and is clear of the firing mechanism? It rather looks that with this revolver, with which this occurrence is concerned, after the time the first shot had been fired something happened to press in a less degree this trigger before it was finally exploded?—The cylinder was moved either by pulling the trigger or by hand.

It might have been done in many ways, but if the pressure was not enough to fire the revolver at first, the effect would be to turn this cylinder round?—Yes. It would keep spinning round.

And you know in this case that the cylinder had somehow or another been rotated so that one cylinder had been missed? —Yes.

Suppose a person had got the revolver and another person came and there was a struggle, it is extremely likely that if they continued to struggle and the revolver was loaded, it would go off?—Yes.

And it is quite impossible for anyone who was not there to know exactly how the revolver in those circumstances would go off?—Yes.

It must be speculation?—Unless you have a wound which will give the explanation.

And if the revolver were between three to six inches from one of them, and one person had it in his hand and the other person seized it, and the revolver was pointing towards him, it is certain it would go off if it were pressed hard enough?—Yes.

And if he happened to be there opposite the revolver it is certain he would be killed?—Yes.

Sir Patrick gave an illustration of such a struggle: he handed the revolver to Mr Walter Frampton, and the two counsel engaged in a struggle for it.

SIR PERCIVAL CLARKE (*interrupting*): That presupposes that the hand holding the revolver has the finger on the trigger?—Yes, the trigger must be pulled.

MR JUSTICE HUMPHREYS: It presupposes two things – the hand holding the revolver is not the hand of the person killed, and the finger of the person not killed is on the trigger.

SIR PATRICK HASTINGS: Or the thumb.

MR JUSTICE HUMPHREYS: Yes.

SIR PATRICK HASTINGS: If two people were struggling to get possession of a revolver, and the pressure exerted was not strong enough to fire it at first, the cylinder might be turned around?

THE WITNESS: It might spin round.

If the struggling persons are close and one has the revolver in her hand, and the other seizes the hand, it would go off?—It might.

When the finger, not of the person killed, is on the trigger?—Yes.

MAJOR HUGH POLLARD, *an expert in firearms, stated that when the revolver was fired, there was an escape of gas between the cylinder and the base of the barrel. He had fired a similar pistol with his left hand gloved and held over the barrel, and there was substantial blackening of the glove.*

You mean that if one puts one's hand over the barrel of a revolver when it is fired it gets black?—Yes.

How recently had the revolver in question been fired?—I cannot say, but it was within a month.

This concluded the case for the Crown.

EVIDENCE FOR THE DEFENCE

SIR PATRICK HASTINGS: My Lord, I understand that the

prison doctor has made a report. By the courtesy of the Prosecution, I have been allowed to see it, and without treating the doctor as a witness for the Defence, I propose to call him.

MR JUSTICE HUMPHREYS: To avoid misunderstanding in future cases, it should be made plain that all reports of prison doctors are confidential. They are often shown to counsel, but it must not be assumed that they are public property which can be called for.

DR J. H. MORTON: I am Governor and Medical Officer of Holloway Prison. I examined Mrs Barney soon after she was admitted.

SIR PATRICK HASTINGS: Did you find on her arms any bruises?—I did. On the left forearm there was a bruise one inch by one inch. On the left upper arm there were three bruises on the outside and one on the inside.

Did they appear to have been caused by Mrs Barney being roughly held by a human hand?—They might have been caused by fingers. On the right forearm there were two small bruises and on the right upper arm a large bruise of later date. There were also recent marks on the right thigh.

Were those marks consistent with the prisoner having been engaged in a violent struggle?—I cannot say; there were other injuries.

What other injuries?—She had a small abrasion at the base of the middle-finger of the left hand. She has that still. There was a small scratch on the finger, and on the margin of the thumb-nail a little bit of the skin had been removed. Another small abrasion was on her little finger.

If she had been struggling with a revolver in her hand, would the marks be consistent with that?—Yes.

The revolver was handed to the witness, who examined it and said that it was possible for the 'sight' to have done some of the damage; the trigger-guard might have caused some of the bruises.

Has there been, while the prisoner has been under your charge, the slightest indication that she has ever been addicted to drugs?—No.

Cross-examined by SIR PERCIVAL CLARKE:

When did you examine Mrs Barney?—Two days after she came to the prison. The oldest marks were those on the left arm.

Might they have been caused if a woman were being restrained by police officers?—No; the marks on people who have been restrained by police officers have been very much more.

MR JUSTICE HUMPHREYS: We had better not pursue this; it would only mean recalling the police officers.

SIR PERCIVAL CLARKE: When do you think the bruises were made?—I should think six or seven days before I saw her. That on the thigh was probably done two or three days before I saw her.

MR JUSTICE HUMPHREYS: Was she at large then?

SIR PERCIVAL CLARKE: Yes, until 3 June.

SIR PATRICK HASTINGS: My Lord, I now propose to call the prisoner.

The prisoner was duly sworn in.

MR JUSTICE HUMPHREYS: You may be seated if you wish.

MRS BARNEY, *accompanied by two wardresses, then gave her evidence seated.*

SIR PATRICK HASTINGS: You are 26 years of age and the daughter of Sir John and Lady Mullens?—Yes.

On 2 August 1928, did you marry John Sterling Barney, an American, of New York?—Yes.

Can you in a sentence tell the court how your husband treated you?—He was very unkind.

Were there numerous occasions on which you were subjected to physical violence?—Yes.

Even in your parents' house?—Yes.

Did he leave you in 1930?—Yes.

With the assistance of your mother, have you taken the best legal advice as to whether or not you could divorce him, and have you been advised that the difficulty in this country is that your husband being an American, you are a domiciled American?—Yes.

And you have been unable to divorce him?—Yes.

You have a private income of your own, and from the day

you took the premises in the mews have you lived there
continuously except for holidays?—Yes.

When did you first meet the man who is dead, Michael
Stephen?—Some time ago. Just once in Paris. I did not see
him again after that for a considerable time.

In the autumn of last year did he come unexpectedly to
your flat and call upon you?—Yes.

Were you alone then?—Yes.

Michael Stephen, having come and reintroduced himself
to you, did from that time become extremely friendly?—
Yes.

Did you become very devoted to him and were you anxious
to marry him?—Very.

For reasons you have given me, that was impossible?—Yes.

You have told us you were devoted to him. In fact, had he
any means, so far as you know, of earning his own living?—
No.

From the time you became devoted to him did you in fact
become his mistress?—Yes.

At the time that you became devoted to him, did you
support him almost entirely?—Almost entirely.

We have heard he got a little money sometimes from his
mother. Had he any other source of income?—No.

Were you very anxious to keep what was then your mode
of life from your mother and father?—Yes.

Was Michael Stephen always kind to you?—Not always.

Were you occasionally frightened of him?—Yes.

On at least one occasion were you so frightened that you
communicated with the police?—Yes.

Did a police officer come to your flat?—Yes.

I don't know what the suggestion is underlying the police
telephone number by your bed, but why did you put it
there?—The windows of the house were near the ground
and I was afraid, as I was alone.

Why is Michael Stephen's letter signed 'Mickesh'?—That
is just the way he spelt 'Mickey'.

Mickey is the name you used to call him?—Yes.

Have you ever called Michael Stephen 'Chicken' in your
life?—No.

And until Mrs Hall stated that you called out : 'Chicken, Chicken,' have you ever called anybody 'Chicken'?—No.

Michael Stephen was frequently in your flat at all hours of the day and night?—Yes.

When you wrote in your letter: 'I adore it when you are sweet and kind to me, as I haven't had a lot of affection in my life as you have had,' to what were you referring?—Chiefly to my married life.

You also wrote: 'I feel like suicide when you are angry.' Had you ever spoken to Michael Stephen about suicide?—Yes.

Why had you told him anything about suicide?—Because he made me so unhappy at times.

'Sometimes when you are feeling furious, do try to think of the hell I had to endure with J.B.' Who is J.B.?—My husband.

Did that letter express your genuine feelings?—Yes.

I want to ask a question or two about some of the causes of unhappiness between you and Michael. Used he to gamble? —Yes.

Was there a particular person with whom he used to gamble? —Yes.

A man or a woman?—A woman.

Did you approve of or like his going out to gamble with that woman?—No.

Why not?—Because it was very bad for him; he could not afford it.

And when he wanted money to gamble with, whom did he come and ask for it?—He asked me.

When he wrote in his letter: 'Forgive me all the dreadful, horrible things I've done and I promise to be better and kinder,' do you know exactly what he was referring to?— Partly that he'd been out gambling with this woman.

And when he insisted on doing that did it cause scenes between you?—Yes.

And have there been a number of occasions on which you and he have quarrelled?—Yes.

In spite of all that, did you remain right up to the end absolutely devoted to him?—Yes.

Do you remember the night in May when there was a discussion with the taxi-cabman at the door?—Yes.

And after you had gone to your room, did Michael come to the mews and call to you?—Yes.

Had you seen him earlier?—Yes.

Had he asked you for money?—Yes.

Did you give him any?—I did, but he said it was not enough.

When he came back, did he ask for more?—Yes.

In the house was there a revolver?—Yes.

Whose was it?—Mine.

How long had you had it?—Eight or nine years.

From whom did you get it?—A Captain Coler.

Where were you living?—I was staying with him and his wife in Devonshire.

Had there been any sort of sport or game that you had indulged in?—We had been rabbit shooting. We very often went out in the car at night and shot rabbits by the aid of the headlights.

While you were in Devonshire, did you ever fire the revolver?—I fired it in some woods.

Had you ever fired a revolver before?—No.

Until you came to your flat did you ever fire it again?—Never.

Why did you take it to the flat?—I moved everything from Belgrave Square.

When you were first in the mews, where did you keep the revolver?—In a room at the back of the bed.

When did you load it?

MR JUSTICE HUMPHREYS: She has not told us where she got the ammunition from.

SIR PATRICK HASTINGS: Where did you get the ammunition?—Captain Coler gave me the revolver and the ammunition.

When did you load the revolver?—Very soon after I moved to the flat.

Was it always loaded?—Yes.

Do you remember finding anything in the revolver when you loaded it?—An empty cartridge, which I put in a cardboard box.

How many times has that revolver been fired while you were in the flat?—Once.

When Stephen came to your window in May and asked for money, what did you say or do?—He stayed outside the house for some time.

Do you remember what you did?—I was so unhappy that I thought I would make him think I was going to commit suicide. I got the revolver and fired at random. I thought he would think I had killed myself, and would fetch people, the police possibly, so I looked out of the window and he saw me and realised, I suppose, that I was all right, and nothing more was said or done at the time.

On the left wall of your bedroom are the marks of a revolver bullet. When were they made?—On that occasion.

Was that the only occasion you fired the revolver before the day of Stephen's death?—Yes.

I want now to go straight to the occurrence of 31 May. I think you had had a number of friends in the afternoon for what has been described as a 'cocktail party'?—Yes.

And Michael Stephen, I gather, was there, and after it was over you and he and one of the witnesses went out to dinner at the Café de Paris?—Yes.

Who paid?—I did.

Did you afterwards go to the club which has been mentioned and stay there for some time?—Yes.

And when you left the club, did you go back to the flat? —Yes.

On what terms were you with Michael Stephen when you returned to the flat?—Friendly.

I am afraid you must tell us this, Mrs Barney. Where did you go when you came back to the flat?—We went into the bedroom.

And at first, while you were in your room, was Michael Stephen kind to you, or was he not?—First of all, yes.

And what happened after you had been there for some time? Did he continue kind? Just tell us what he said to show how he changed.—He made love to me but was very angry because I did not respond in the way he wanted, and he said perhaps my feelings had changed. I told him that it was only because I was so unhappy at what had happened during the day – about money – and I could not forget it. That made him all the more angry. He said he was not pleased with the way things were going, and he wanted to go out the next day and not see me at all.

In other words, he was not either loving or kind at that time?—No.

What did Stephen do – did he stop in bed or get up?—He got up after some time. He dressed. I asked him not to leave me. I said if he did I should kill myself.

When you said you would kill yourself, did he say or do anything?—Yes, he got up from the dressing-table and made a dash for the armchair, and said: 'Well, anyway, you won't do it with this.'

Do you know how he knew the revolver was there?—I don't know exactly how, but he knew everything.

When he said: 'You won't do it with this,' what did he do?—He picked up the revolver. He ran out of the room towards the spare room. I ran after him.

At that time in whose hand was the revolver?—Michael's.

Did you come up to him?—Yes. In the doorway of the spare room.

Will you now tell us as much as you can remember of what then happened?—We struggled with the revolver. He had it and I wanted it back. I kept saying: 'Give it to me.' I don't know whether he said, 'No', but the more I tried, the more he tried to get it away. The struggle became more and more hard. We were moving about. I cannot remember all our positions. I was so unhappy. I was crying. I don't remember, but I know we were struggling and suddenly I heard a shot.

Stop there. Have you ever in your life desired to shoot Michael Stephen?—Never.

Has there ever been in your life anybody you were fonder of than Michael Stephen?—Never.

Did you shoot him that night?—No.

Had you any motive for shooting him?—None.

When you heard the revolver go off, did you know he had been shot?—No.

What did he do?—He just looked at me with an expression – the only word I can think of is astonishment.

Did he stay where he was?—He went a few steps into the bathroom.

Had you the slightest idea that moment that he had been shot?—None whatsoever.

How long was he in the bathroom?—Only a minute or two.

What did he do?—Half-opened the door, which he had more or less closed behind him, and said: 'Go quickly, fetch a doctor' or: 'Better fetch a doctor.'

Was that the first time you had any indication he was hurt?—Yes.

When did you first realise that he was dangerously hurt?— When I came upstairs after 'phoning the doctor.

What was he doing?—Half-sitting and half-lying.

Are you able to tell us how long he lived?—It seemed hours to me, but he seemed to me to live until just before the doctor came. I made a remark to him which I thought he understood just at the last.

Until he died, you were looking after him?—Yes.

What were you doing?—Everything I could think of. I did not know what to do, but I did the only things I could think of.

Did he speak to you at all?—Yes.

What did he say?—He said, 'I wish the doctor would hurry. I wish to tell him it was an accident. It was not your fault.' He said that over and over again.

MRS BARNEY *then broke down and wept. When she had recovered, she stated that she remembered very little of what she had said to Dr Durrant or the police.*

One of the police officers says that you struck him in the face?—I don't remember it. I was told about it.

When you were taken to the police station, do you remember making a statement to one of the police officers, and is there a single word of that statement that is not true? —No, excepting that I made it under conditions in which my mother and father were present, and I did not say things I hoped they would not have to know.

Did you mother and father know of the terms on which you had been living?—No.

Before you made that statement, did you ask anyone's advice as to whether it was wise or unwise to make it?—No.

And did you make it because you wished to make it, and was it true?—Yes.

Cross-examined by SIR PERCIVAL CLARKE:

Had the disagreement between you throughout the day been with regard to this other woman?—To a certain extent.

Was it a woman for whom Michael had developed some affection?—He was fond of her.

When he said he was going to leave you, did you think he was going to leave you for this other woman?—I did not think that.

Who did you think was going to keep him?—I thought he would probably try to keep himself by gambling. He thought he was very successful at it.

Did he ever tell anyone he was very fond of this other woman?—That he was fond of her, yes.

And you, I suppose, were very anxious that he should not leave you for her?—Well, I did not think he was going to leave me for her.

You were very much in love with him?—Yes.

Were you jealous of him looking at and speaking to other women?—No.

Was that not the cause of your frequent quarrels?—No.

Was the cause of your quarrels always money?—Yes, money and his gambling habits, in which the woman encouraged him.

There was a woman in the case, however?—Oh, yes.

Did he see a good deal of her?—Not a good deal. Just occasionally.

And that was the only woman, so far as you know?—Yes.

Were the quarrels you had with him frequent?—They were not so many. They happened from time to time, but we made them up and were perfectly happy.

Did they generally occur in the small hours of the morning in Williams Mews?—Yes.

I daresay you would raise your voice and he would raise

F

his sufficiently loud for the neighbours to hear?—Probably.

Have you got, generally speaking, full control of your temper?—Yes.

Were you not quick to resent interference?—I don't quite understand.

Were you quick to take offence if anything happened of which you did not approve?—I don't quite understand what you are driving at.

For instance, when Inspector Campion was in the room, you struck him a violent blow in the face.—I do not remember.

Had you lost your temper?—I was very unhappy. I was frenzied.

Would it be true to say that you accompanied the blow with the words: 'I will teach you to say you will put me in a cell, you vile swine'?—That also I don't remember. I was told that I had said it.

MRS BARNEY *said that she did not know where the man who gave her the revolver now lived.* SIR PATRICK HASTINGS *pointed out that he was at the moment present in court.*

MRS BARNEY *went on to say that the one shot fired in Devonshire was the extent of her experience of firearms. Apart from the other two shots of which she had spoken, it was the only one she had fired from that pistol. She had no other pistol at Williams Mews.*

SIR PERCIVAL CLARKE: Tell us about the incident on the night of 19 May—I had given all the money I had to Michael, and when I got home alone I had no money to pay the taxi-cab. I told the driver I was sorry and asked him to come back the next day, which he did. I did not think it was as late as 3 am, but it might have been. Afterwards, Michael arrived in a taxi-cab and asked for money, which I declined to give him, as I had not any. He went away and shortly afterwards came back and rang my bell. I looked out to see who it was.

Did you tell him to go away or you would fetch the police?—Yes.

Did he tell you that you could fetch them, but he would wait?—Words to that effect.

Did you say anything like: 'Laugh, baby; laugh for the last time?'—I said: 'Smile, baby, now smile.'

'For the last time?'—No, I don't remember saying that. I don't think I did.

Were you at that time undressed?—I was in a dressing-gown.

Was the next thing that happened your firing of a pistol? —Not actually the next thing. When I spoke to him I was looking out of the window, and the next thing was I went back into the room to get the revolver.

What for?—I wanted him to think I was going to kill myself. I was so unhappy.

Just play-acting?—Up to a point, yes.

If you wanted him to think you were going to commit suicide, are you sure you did not say: 'Laugh for the last time?'—I said 'smile' because all the evening he had been smiling and sneering. He seemed so indifferent, I thought I would tell him to 'smile now' and he would realise I was going to do something desperate to myself.

You were at the window when you were speaking to him? —Yes.

Were you not at the window when you fired the pistol?— No.

Did you not immediately afterwards fall, or pretend to fall?—No.

You were not aware that someone was looking at you from nearly opposite?—I was not.

How was it that the bullet hit the wall at such an angle as to ricochet into the furniture?—I fired in the room itself.

Were you near enough for anyone to see the flash or smoke?—Possibly. The room is very small.

Do you know what became of him after you fired?—Yes, I continued to look out of the window because I did not want him to think that I was dead and go to the police. After the shot had subsided a little while, I looked out of the window to let him know I was all right.

Did you know that he got into a greengrocer's van?—He told me the next day he had been home.

Was not his home with you?—No.

Did he not keep his clothes at your flat?—No.

Did you ever throw his clothes out of the window after him?—No.

You saw him later on 19 May, and were you quite friendly again?—Yes. We made it up on the telephone and he came round early that morning.

Did the quarrels continue until 30 May?—No, there was nothing serious between that incident until the luncheon on the day of the cocktail party.

On that evening did Michael Stephen go away for a little time with a woman he wanted to gamble with – a Miss 'C'?— I don't know who you mean.

Very well, I will not mention the name. Did the dispute about the gambling continue after you had got back that night and had gone to bed?—Yes.

And did the dispute involve the raising of voices?—Yes.

That would be heard in the mews?—I suppose so.

Were you hysterical, and did you call out loudly and scream?—Towards the end, yes.

At that time did he get up?—Yes, and it was while he was dressing that I really began to get hysterical.

He was, as I understand, going to leave you then?—He said he was.

And that, with your affection for him, troubled you very much?—Yes. I was crying and very unhappy. I asked him not to leave me.

I understand you told him that if he did you would commit suicide. Did you genuinely intend to do that, or was that also play-acting?—I intended to do it.

Did you say: 'Get out, I'll shoot you, I'll shoot you'?

SIR PATRICK HASTINGS *protested that the words were 'I'll shoot', and not 'I'll shoot you'. The prisoner stated that what she remembered saying was: 'Don't leave me, don't leave me. If you do, I'll shoot myself.'*

SIR PERCIVAL CLARKE: You mentioned the word 'shoot' loud enough for anyone to hear?—Yes.

Was anything else said by either of you?—When I said I would shoot myself, he said: 'Anyway, you won't do it with this.'

I put it to you that you told him to get out of the house?—
I wanted him to stay. I did not want him to go.

No, but you thought he was going, and you did not want
him to go to some other woman?—Not to some other woman;
but I knew that if he went he would be gambling and get
into a lot of things which would involve him in a lot of
trouble.

Did you hear Dr Durrant say that you told him Michael
said he would go to the other woman?—There was a question
about that, of course, because he used to visit her and play
bridge with her, but I did not think he would leave me for
her.

I suggest to you there were other people not quite so
excited who were listening, and that you told him to get out,
saying: 'I will shoot, I will shoot'?—No, I did not say 'Get
out'.

Did he then say he would be going, and was the next thing
that happened the firing of the shot?—No.

Well, what was the next thing that happened?—The
struggle.

Whose finger was it that was on the trigger when the shot
was fired?—I have no idea.

Did he pick up the pistol, and which hand was it in when
you were trying to get it away from him?—I do not know.

Cannot you give us any explanation as to how that pistol
was fired?—In the struggle we were moving about continuously, and I do not know who held the revolver.

Yes, but it was not going off continuously. You heard it go
off, and I want to know in whose hand it was when it went
off.—I don't remember.

I put it to you that it would be quite impossible for him to
have had that pistol pointing towards himself, to have pulled
the trigger and exploded the cartridge. You don't suggest he
did that, do you?—No.

He had no wish to end his life, as far as you know?—No.

Is it your theory that you were holding the stock of the
pistol and your finger was on the trigger, and in the struggle
he forced your finger back and made it fire?—I have no
theory.

What happened to the pistol when the shot was fired?—I do not know.

Did the pistol fall to the ground?—I do not remember hearing it, but eventually I did see it on the ground.

You cannot say whether it fell from your hand or not?—No.

Had you got it, or nearly got it, away from him?—No.

Was he holding it when it was fired?—I don't remember, but I think so.

There were no marks of any blackness on his hands?—No.

Directly it was fired did he say: 'What have you done?'—No.

What did he say?—He did not say one word until he said from the bathroom: 'Fetch a doctor.'

Are you sufficiently clear in mind to know whether he said it or not?—After the shot was fired, yes.

You said: 'Mickey, Mickey, come back to me'?—Not then.

After a short space of time did you say: 'I will do anything you want me to'?—Nothing of the sort, because when he told me to fetch a doctor I went straight to the telephone.

You were not calm and collected?—No.

Probably you do not remember the words overheard by Mrs Hall when you telephoned to the doctor. Did you tell him someone had shot himself?—Yes.

Did you say over the telephone anything about your having any part in it?—No.

Did you say: 'Come back Michael'?—I cannot remember, but in my frantic state I might have said it.

Questioned about the mark on the bedroom wall, the defendant said she could not recall whether she mentioned it to Dr Durrant or whether he saw it and asked about it.

You employ a woman to clean your flat?—Yes.

Was there any other person in the habit of going to your bedroom?—No one, except Michael.

Had the mark been on the wall some time, the cleaning woman would have noticed it?—She did.

Did you speak about it?—The day after it happened.

Do you know sufficient about the revolver to know that if it were held in the course of a struggle in any way by the chamber it would not fire?—I do not.

You do not know whether it was in his hand or yours or from whose hand it fell?—No.

Following up, in your anger with him, because he was going to leave you, you said: 'Get out. I will shoot', and you shot?—No.

Re-examined by SIR PATRICK HASTINGS:

Have you ever in your life said that you would shoot Michael?—No.

Have you said you would shoot yourself?—Yes.

A question has been asked as to the genuineness of your feeling. In fact, did you instruct a firm of solicitors, Messrs Graham & Co, to make a will some short time before this occurrence?—Yes.

Leaving everything you had to someone?—Yes.

Who was it?—Michael.

I want that revolver placed on the ledge in front of the witness.

The revolver was placed on the ledge of the witness box.

Will you be good enough to stand, Mrs Barney. Pick up that revolver.

The defendant picked up the revolver with her right hand.

Have you ever picked up a revolver with your left hand in your life?—No.

Are you left-handed?—No.

That is my case.

MR JUSTICE HUMPHREYS *asked the defendant whether, when her friend gave her the revolver, he also gave her the cartridges. The defendant said that he did, and that they were in the box.*

MR JUSTICE HUMPHREYS: Did your friend tell you that you had no right to have a revolver unless you had a firearms certificate?—No.

And he is a captain in the army?—Yes.

The defendant then left the witness box.

CLOSING SPEECH FOR THE CROWN

SIR PERCIVAL CLARKE *began by reminding the jury that three cartridges had been fired:*

There is no support whatever in evidence that the cartridge which was found in the cartridge box was one which was fired six or seven years ago. It was said by Mrs Barney that that was when it was done, but that is all the evidence you have about it. I suggest to you that that was the shot that was fired out of the window in the early morning of 19 May.

Undoubtedly, the cause of the trouble was some other woman. It has now been sought to say that the subject of the quarrel was Stephen's gambling with Mrs Barney's money. No motive is sufficient to justify such an act, but motive may explain it, and I suggest to you that there is no motive more forceful or powerful than jealousy for doing things, the consequence of which one may not at the moment appreciate but which brings sorrow afterwards. There were only two persons in the room on that fateful night, and by one of them no evidence can be given.

From the other fell evidence which she had a very strong reason for colouring to make it appear that no crime had been committed by her. There had been wrangling in bed and the man had said that he would get up and leave her— leave her for that other woman. What is more likely to make a woman lose her temper and control of herself? The prisoner's story that the man picked up the revolver is uncorroborated, and there is not the slightest doubt that the revolver, when it was fired, was in the prisoner's hand and that it was her finger which was on the trigger. To fire it presented no great difficulty, and it has been admitted that if the cylinder was held the weapon could not be fired.

If there was a struggle for the revolver, Michael Stephen's hand was on the weapon, he knew it was there and that it was loaded and he had no desire to end his life. He was not likely to point it at himself; indeed, pointing in the direction in which it was, at that short distance from his coat, it was impossible for him to fire it. Common sense will tell you that the woman had the revolver and there was only room for one finger on the trigger. What reason was there to exert all the pressure that was required to fire the weapon? It was suggested that she had it somehow forced back. Why then was there not the slightest mark on the man's hand, the linen of his shirt-sleeve, or the sleeve of his coat? There is nothing whatever to show that his hand was touching it when the revolver was fired. A point was made about the cleanliness of the hand of the deceased man: if he had been touching the revolver when it was fired, his hand must have been blackened.

If you accept Sir Patrick Hastings' theory that the prisoner had the revolver by the stock, and that the man pressed it in such a way that she involuntarily fired within three or four inches of his body, it would be surprising if he kept his hand by his side all the time. It is evident that the prisoner lost absolute control of herself, and Mrs Hall's recollection was right when, attracted by the shouting and screaming, the windows being open, she heard the prisoner say: 'Get out, get out; I will shoot, I will shoot.' Such a thing might well be said by a jealous woman who thought that her lover was going to leave her. If you accept that, there is an end to any suggestion of accident or that the man fired the revolver himself.

When the shot was fired something had to be done. The man was mortally wounded, and, after saying : 'Good God, what have you done?' he asked the prisoner to call a doctor. When the doctor came, the prisoner could give him no coherent account of what had taken place. She has had food for reflection on many occasions since, but has not given an account of what really happened. Her condition of mind is clearly indicated. Hers is an impossible story. Everything points to the fact that she believed her lover was going to some other- woman, that she felt it so deeply that she would commit suicide if he went, and that she fired in that attitude of minds towards him, which amounts in law to murder. If you believe the prisoner, you must acquit her, but if you weigh the evidence carefully and dispassionately I submit that there is truth in the accusation made against her.

If Stephen's hand was as close to the revolver as Sir Patrick has suggested, why was there no blackening on the dead man's hand? I suggest that the prisoner's hand was on the pistol and her finger was on the trigger when it was fired, and that it was in consequence of the jealous feelings that she had that she uttered the warning threats and fired the shot.

If you are satisfied that the Prosecution have not brought home to her the guilt, no one will be more happy than you to say so in your verdict—but if, on the other hand, looking at the weapon, the cleanliness of the hands, the threats, the continual quarrels and the subject of them, you are satisfied that there is no doubt in your minds of the prisoner's guilt, you will say so.

At the conclusion of SIR PERCIVAL CLARKE's *speech,* MR JUSTICE HUMPHREYS *asked* SIR PATRICK HASTINGS *whether he wished to address the jury before adjournment.* SIR PATRICK *said that he would if his Lordship would sit to finish the case that day.* MR JUSTICE HUMPHREYS *said he did not think that could be done, whereupon* SIR PATRICK *said that he preferred to address the jury in the morning.*

THIRD DAY   *Wednesday, 6 July*

CLOSING SPEECH FOR THE DEFENCE

SIR PATRICK HASTINGS:

This is the first opportunity that any of us on behalf of the Defence have had of putting the case before you on grounds which we are going to submit make a verdict in the lady's favour inevitable.

Having regard to the terrible position of the lady I represent, I know you will not grudge me a little time to put forward the other side of the case. I shall not indulge in flights of oratory or dramatic surprises, supposed to be the attributes of an advocate. They may be amusing, but we are not in this court to be amused. We leave that to the people who have been here the last two or three days, no doubt enjoying and gloating over every expression of agony; the distinguished authors here to see that people outside not sufficiently fortunate to join in the amusement should not miss the slightest sign of the things these distinguished gentlemen can show them. We rather despise some of the people here and loathe these things. If they expect to find amusement here, they will not find it from me.

In this case, so anxious am I that no possible point shall be overlooked, I have done a thing which I do not think I have ever done before during my career at the Bar. I have made a note of everything which has been said, so as to ensure that nothing shall be forgotten.

I was most struck by things which fell from Sir Percival Clarke in opening the case. The first one I noticed was at the very beginning of his speech, when he described Mrs Barney as being a lady who lived in an extravagantly converted flat in the mews. Now I wondered why it was necessary to discuss this extravagantly furnished flat.

What exactly was the evidence on that point? It was that upstairs in the spare room there was practically no furniture at all; in the bedroom there was a divan—a very simple piece of furniture, the sort of thing one would expect in a very small flat—three chairs, two of which were very small, and the third of which was a rather old armchair; downstairs there was very little furniture. That was the extravagantly furnished flat in which Mrs Barney lived.

The next thing was rather more dangerous. Mrs Barney, who, as you know, on the occasion when the police came to her flat, was in a state bordering on frenzy and despair, was stated to have struck one of the police officers in the face. You were told that that matter was put before you that you might see the sort of temper that Mrs Barney gave way to on slight provocation. The provocation was that a young woman was alone in a flat with, within a few yards of her, the man whom she obviously loved lying dead; she was surrounded by police officers who were proposing to remove her to the police station. Sir Percival Clarke says that this is slight provocation. I wonder what Sir Percival Clarke would think is a serious provocation.

Thirdly, there was something much more serious. Three times in the course of his opening speech Sir Percival Clarke said dramatically that Mrs Barney had been heard to say: 'I will shoot you.' In fact, not one single witness said anything of the sort. As the question in this case is whether what was said in evidence and in Mrs Barney's statements—namely, that Stephen had feared lest she might shoot herself—is true, it is unfortunate that you should have been told no less than three times that she was heard to say: 'I will shoot you', when not one living soul was going to say anything of the sort. You must not be influenced by the simple and straightforward story which was put before you two days ago, when you know that some parts of it were quite untrue.

There are cases in which advocates appearing for the defence are driven in despair to plead to the jury and to urge that the defendant is entitled to the benefit of the doubt. I am not going to do anything of that sort. I am not going to ask you to give Mrs Barney the benefit of the doubt. I am going to show you that there is no doubt and that there is no evidence on which this woman could be convicted of any offences whatsoever.

We now come to the incidents of 19 May when Mrs Barney is alleged to have shot at Stephen out of her window while he was in the mews. She was not charged with that matter, and it was introduced so that when you considered your verdict, you would remember that on a previous occasion Mrs Barney had tried to murder Stephen, and had shot at him with the intention of hitting him. If there was any evidence of that, the Prosecution would be entitled to rely on it, but you might think that, by introducing it, the Prosecution were bolstering up a non-existent case by something of which there was no evidence.

The Prosecution's story was simple. Stephen came to the flat, asked for money which he did not get, and walked away —then, according to the Crown, Mrs Barney tried to murder him. Evidence was given by people who lived in the mews. Unless the mews is very different from every other small community in the civilised world, the people who live there have been thrilled by what has happened and have talked about it a great deal.

Three people were forthcoming. Mrs Stevens never saw Mrs Barney at the window at all when any shot was fired, and she heard nothing. Mr Kiff, the chauffeur, who lived next door to Mrs Barney, also saw nothing, although he was at his window a few feet from her. Mrs Hall, however, said something quite different. She said that she saw Mrs Barney and also saw something bright in her hand. In fact, the revolver was perfectly black. Mrs Barney said that she had never used her left hand and, in the witness box, when asked to pick up the revolver, she immediately did so with her right hand. It is rather odd that, according to the only person who said that she saw Mrs Barney with the revolver at the window, she had it in her left hand. I don't know whether you noticed that at the conclusion of what must have been a terrible ordeal for her in the witness box, I asked Mrs Barney to stand up and take the revolver. It was the only risk we have taken in this case, but I thought it right to take it. You saw her condition, almost in a state of collapse. You noticed she picked the revolver up like *that* (SIR PATRICK *picked up the revolver with his right hand*). It is odd if the only time that Mrs Barney used her left hand was a time when, it is said, she tried to murder Michael Stephen. Mrs Hall said that there was a puff of smoke when the pistol was fired, but the cartridge that was used did not make any smoke. Mrs Hall said that she saw a flash, but the lights of passing motorcars flashed in every window which they passed. She might have seen such a flash or she might have been mistaken and not seen a flash any more than she saw the smoke.

I do not mean to say anything hard about Mrs Hall, but hers is the only evidence, and there is not one scintilla of evidence besides it.

Very few men of mature age have heard the whistle of a bullet past their heads. In this case no one suggests any such thing. Mrs Hall does not even suggest that Mrs Barney was pointing the revolver at Michael Stephen.

What did he think about it? If you had been shot at would you not have taken to your heels? He knew Mrs Barney, but he walked to her window and said: 'Don't be silly. They are looking at us.' That is the man who, according to Sir Percival, was in imminent danger of being murdered. Then he walked over to Mrs Hall and said: 'I do not think I ought to leave her because I am so afraid she will commit suicide.'

Things grow in people's minds and became magnified by

after-events. Members of the jury, picture the scene for yourselves. If anyone of you thought that a woman was trying to murder a man, you would do something about it. What did these three witnesses do? They all went back to bed, and the next morning, living though they did in a part of London where policemen were not entirely absent, and police stations existed, they said not a word to anybody. Can you imagine that chauffeur and those chauffeurs' wives not telling someone if they thought for a moment that a revolver had been fired out of the window?

Moreover, the police have searched the mews with a comb to see if they could find the spot where the bullet hit the wall, and they found nothing. No one heard the bullet, no one saw it, no one has ever been able to trace it, and, if you eliminate the enthusiastic Mrs Hall, there is no evidence that Mrs Barney ever fired at the man she adored. And next morning Mrs Barney and Michael were together, the best of friends. I ask you to say that, with regard to this matter there is absolutely no evidence at all.

Let us now turn to the events of 31 May. In a court of law, cocktail parties sound so dreadful. But people do have them. I dare say that quite a number of those who have listened so enthusiastically to the case with no other object than to be amused have been to cocktail parties. The cocktail party that took place in Mrs Barney's flat on the afternoon of 31 May does not matter. Nothing relevant occurred until Mrs Barney and Stephen returned to the flat at night.

On that night of the murder, no one *saw* anything, but it has been suggested that three people *heard* something. Mrs Hall was twenty yards away and she had a crying baby in the room. Her husband was with her at her window, but he has not been called by the Crown, and, presumably, he heard nothing. The curtains of Mrs Barney's bedroom were thick and heavy and they were closely drawn, but Mrs Hall said that, in those circumstances, she heard Mrs Barney say: 'I am going to shoot'; Stephen said: 'Good God what have you done?' and Mrs Barney said: 'Chicken, chicken, don't leave me.' I do not care if Mrs Hall heard every one of those things because they are quite consistent with the case for the

Defence. But has anyone any doubt that Mrs Barney did not say anything of the sort? She had never called Stephen 'Chicken' in her life. She had called him 'Mickey', but Mrs Hall was sure that she said 'Chicken'. She was as sure of that as of the puff of smoke on 19 May. Mrs Hall should be a little more careful and think a little before she is prepared to be so definite about things which might be important. No one else heard 'I am going to shoot' or 'Chicken, chicken, don't leave me.'

Mr Kiff heard nothing except the shot, but Mrs Stevens did hear something. You can see the picture of the various wives in this mews. For the first time Williams Mews became the centre of interest to journalists and policemen, and apparently Mrs Stevens and Mrs Hall were not on the best of terms. When Mrs Hall informed the police of what she had heard, and Mrs Stevens unfortunately had heard nothing, Mrs Stevens at least had the satisfaction of knowing: 'Well, if the police are going to credit Mrs Hall with hearing what I did not, then the police must credit me with hearing what Mrs Hall did not. She only heard two revolver shots. I heard seven. One, months before. One, on 19 May, and, on the night of 31 May, no less than five.' Those five shots were a little too much even for the Prosecution, and they were driven to introduce Mr Kiff and extract from him the inform-ation that on that night he had thrown a piece of gas-iron at a cat that was making a noise, that that gas-iron had gone bouncing about the mews, and that that might have created the noise which Mrs Stevens thought was that of shots.

Unfortunately for the Prosecution, Mr Kiff did not throw the gas-iron at the cat until some 20 minutes after Mrs Stevens had heard the fusillade which she came to court so proudly to describe. I would like to warn Mrs Stevens as I warned Mrs Hall, because a woman who gives evidence like that is dangerous. It would be awful if the life of any one of those in court depended on the evidence of a woman like that. In the police court Mrs Stevens said nothing about hearing Stephen say: 'God God, what have you done?' but she is now prepared to say that she had heard that.

Dr Durrant, the main witness for the Prosecution, said

that he found Mrs Barney utterly distraught. He painted a picture which you may think was one of the most tragic that you have ever heard. Mrs Barney adored Stephen. The only thing she begged the police to do was to let her go and kiss him when he was dead, before she went to the police station. Why they did not allow her to do that I do not know. Mrs Barney told the doctor what had happened within a few minutes of the tragedy. She told him that Stephen had got very angry and said that he would go to the other woman, that he then dressed, that she threatened to commit suicide if he left her, that he took the revolver, and that a struggle ensued during which the revolver went off. It must have been an unbelievably awful moment in a woman's life. Dr Durrant said that she happened to be passionately devoted to the dead man. She may be a good actress—as good an actress, perhaps, as some of those now in court—but was she acting when she said that she was devoted to him?

Then I asked Dr Durrant a question which might have had the most awful result. I asked him whether, in his opinion, Mrs Barney was in such a mental condition that she could possibly have invented the story she told, and the doctor said 'No'. 'Did you believe that she was telling the truth?' I asked, and the doctor said 'Yes'.

Inspector Winter later searched the flat and found two letters. In one, written by Stephen to Mrs Barney, he said: 'Forgive me all the dreadful horrible things I have done, baby. I promise to be better and kinder so that you won't be frightened any more.' That was written by the man who had been terribly unkind to her, who was living on her and was going to her for money. If ever there was a pathetic document it was her answer in which she said: 'I adore it when you are sweet and kind to me, as I have not had a lot of affection in my life as you have had . . . So you see it means a great deal and I feel like suicide when you are angry.' The last sentence of that letter is vitally important.

This revolver is obviously a piece of metal on which the fingerprints of the person who holds it would be there beyond all question. If Mrs Barney's story is untrue she is not a clever woman, she is a lunatic to have invented such a story, because everybody knows that when the police come upon the scene the first thing they do is to ask themselves if the fingerprints of the person whom they are going to charge are upon the revolver.

The fingerprints of Mrs Barney would have been upon that revolver if she had held it. The first thing the inspector did was to take this revolver with the most extreme care and send it to that great department of Scotland Yard, the Finger Print Expert Division. Inspector Winter has said that the marks on the revolver were so blurred that no fingerprints were decipherable except one, his own. What would have been Mrs Barney's position if they had picked up this revolver and found her fingerprints upon it?

Having called attention to the fact that, within a few hours of the tragedy, the defendant made three statements, SIR PATRICK *continued*:

You are asked to give a verdict of guilty of murder against a woman who told that story to all these people, a story that the Prosecution could never suggest has been changed. I do not think that Sir Percival mentioned that, but I am supplementing his speech because of all the diverse things said by witnesses for the Prosecution.

At the beginning of this case I asked for the expert witnesses to be out of court. One does not idly ask that witnesses like Sir Bernard Spilsbury should be out of court.

You may think it was anticipated that some cross-examination might have to be directed to the expert witnesses, but Sir Bernard Spilsbury said nothing that affected my case, so I had no questions to put to him. He gave no indication, not a shadow of evidence, to suggest that this man's death could not have been caused in the way that Mrs Barney has said for weeks that it was caused. It is true that he gave evidence that in his opinion it was not a case of suicide, but no one has ever suggested that it was. That was the only importance of Sir Bernard Spilsbury's evidence, and I am sorry—and I express to him my regret—that I should have asked him to be out of court.

I am sure all of you have said to yourselves: if the Prosecution's story is right, if Sir Bernard Spilsbury's story is right, that this was a strong and muscular man who had not got the revolver himself, would he be likely to allow a small fragile woman to come within three inches of him and shoot him dead? If they had said she shot him from ten feet away, it would be understandable, but their case is that a man of his physique allowed this woman to get within three inches of him, and allowed her to shoot him dead without attempting to get the revolver.

There is no evidence upon which you could be asked to hang a cat. There never was any evidence upon which a woman should be subjected to the misery of being put on trial for her life.

What evidence is there now? Just think what she is going through now: what she has been going through: what the parents must be going through—waiting to know whether she must live or die. And on what evidence? There is none.

Think of a woman in her position. The thought of what every question may mean, and knowing what Sir Percival is going to ask or whether her answers are wise or unwise. Put yourselves in that box with those two wardresses beside you. Would you have given evidence like Mrs Barney, if it were not true? Did Sir Percival catch her out anywhere?

Referring to the evidence that the revolver had a 14lb pull, SIR PATRICK *submitted that it fired very easily. Holding it up before the jury, he clicked the trigger many times with each finger of his right hand.*

Sir Bernard Spilsbury said that if he put the revolver in a certain position he could not fire it. May I say that if I put the revolver here (*on the desk in front of him*) I cannot fire it with my foot. If anybody had said it would not be likely to go off, I should have asked them to load the revolver, take a court usher, and struggle with him to get possession of it. Do you think he would have said it was quite safe? He would have said: 'No, thank you. Let two ushers go and struggle, not me.' Do you think there is any doubt that if two people struggled for this revolver it is bound to go off?

This has been an awful experience for you, members of the jury, just as it has been awful for all of us who are concerned in this case—awful to see a woman tortured like this, awful to see her parents tortured like this. It is impossible to think what the last two days have meant to them and what the next few hours mean. But I must not emphasise that. We have got our duty to do.

Mrs Barney seems to have had a tragic life: tied to an American, a brute, whom she cannot divorce. Whatever may have been the character of this man who is dead, she loved him. She has not been very fortunate in the people whom she has met in her life.

I am not going to ask you for the benefit of the doubt. I am not going to beg for mercy and a lenient view of what has happened. I stand here and I claim of you that on the evidence that has been put before you, Mrs Barney is entitled as a right to a verdict in her favour. She is a young woman with the whole of her life before her. I beg you to remember that, and I ask of you as a matter of justice and as of right that you should set her free.

THE SUMMING-UP

After describing SIR PERCIVAL CLARKE's *speeches for the Prosecution as 'perfectly fair and temperate'*, MR JUSTICE HUMPHREYS *told the jury*:

You have listened to a remarkable forensic effort this morning. I am not paying compliments when I say that it is certainly one of the finest speeches I myself have ever heard at the Bar in the course of a somewhat protracted experience. It is of all the more assistance to you because it consisted of a careful and accurate analysis of the evidence.

This is a case which has apparently excited great interest among a number of people. It had been written about long before it arrived at this court in a number of newspapers of varying degrees of respectability. I myself had read nothing about this case until I began to read the notes of the evidence.

Some person has thought right—I am not blaming him in any way—to send me at my house cuttings from certain newspapers which publish what profess to be the facts about the woman who is being tried, and broadcast in that way statements about them and their friends and the 'set', as it is called, in which they live. I beg of you, if any of you before you knew you were at all likely to sit upon the jury which would try this woman, have read anything in the newspapers about this case, that you will put such matters entirely out of your mind.

There is one other matter—and it is not by way of criticism of the speech to which you have just listened—but that speech included a number of references in somewhat sneering terms to the Prosecution and the witnesses for the Prosecution. Persons who are called by the Crown in a criminal case are not called because the Crown hope or intend their evidence to procure a verdict in favour of the Prosecution. The duty of the Crown, and it has been well and properly observed in this case, is to call every witness in a criminal case whose evidence is relevant and can throw some light on the transaction.

It has been said that it was cruel, inhuman, that the Crown, the Prosecution, should have put that woman on her trial. She is not here because of any act of that kind, however, but because an experienced magistrate who heard the facts of the case considered that there was a case fit to be considered by a jury; and, secondly, because the grand jury who heard the witnesses in this case considered, as they showed by their action, that they agreed with the magistrate's view that it was a fit and proper case to be tried by a jury. That is why the accused woman is here.

Turning to the law in the case, his Lordship continued as follows:

There are three possible verdicts which you may return: (1) guilty of murder; (2) not guilty of murder but guilty of manslaughter, which is open to you as a matter of law and is clearly a possible verdict on the facts of the case; and (3) not guilty.

I will have something to say on the manslaughter aspect of the case, but as you know, it is a crime of far less degree than murder, and what Mrs Barney is charged with in the indictment is murder. Murder is the unlawful killing of some person with the intention of killing that person, or at least doing that person grievous bodily harm.

In this case the evidence—the undisputed evidence—is that the deceased man died in the early hours of the morning of 31 May as the result of a bullet fired from the revolver which you have seen and which, in due time, I am going to ask you to take to your room and examine for yourselves. That bullet entered the deceased man's left lung, and you have had pointed out to you by Sir Bernard Spilsbury on his own body the exact point where it entered. It went through the lung in a course which was either horizontal or nearly horizontal, and that was the cause of death.

It follows that Mrs Barney is not to be convicted of murder unless it has been proved by the Prosecution by evidence to your satisfaction that she fired that fatal shot, and that she fired it intending at the time to kill the man at whom she was firing. It would be absurd to suppose that if she deliberately fired the revolver at and into the body of the deceased man at the distance of a few inches she desired to do him grievous bodily harm and not to kill him.

You will have two or possibly three questions to consider to satsify yourselves that she fired the shot. It meant, of necessity, that her finger was on the trigger, or that the man's finger was on the trigger and she caused him to pull it. You must be satisfied that she did that intentionally, not accidentally. The Prosecution must prove to your satisfaction, and by proof in a criminal case, this means something more than probability and something more than suspicion. Probability and suspicion will not do: you must be satisfied that the Prosecution has proved, not that it was quite likely that the accused might have murdered the deceased or that it is quite open on the evidence that it might be so; you must be satisfied that she did it.

There is really little dispute that Mrs Barney was the person who fired the shot. She told you, and you may have formed the view that she told you frankly, that she cannot say whether her finger was on the trigger or not. You may think it would not have been difficult for her if she desired to lie to you to say it was the man's finger which was on the trigger, but she did not. She says it was an accidental pressing of the trigger, just as she says she had no intention of injuring the man.

Sir Bernard Spilsbury has demonstrated that it would not

be impossible, but unlikely, that the dead man could have been holding the revolver with his finger on the trigger. Another piece of evidence was that the dead man was a muscular, strong young man, and in the struggle he had assuredly not the slightest desire that the revolver should go off. It is extremely unlikely that he would have put his finger on the trigger.

On the other hand, if he were not holding the revolver with his finger on the trigger, that would leave a space for any finger which might have tried to get hold of it (MR JUSTICE HUMPHREYS *demonstrated with the revolver*).

You may think the most likely, almost the only, way in which the wound can be accounted for is that in the struggle the woman who is on trial somehow got her finger upon and pulled the trigger.

Did she fire the revolver intentionally? If it were true that Mrs Barney pointed the revolver intentionally at the body of the deceased man and then fired it, you would be justified in saying there was only one intention she could have had, because everyone knows that to discharge a revolver at a person three or four inches away is likely to kill him, or at least to endanger his life.

I have to tell you that if you are satisfied on the evidence as a whole that it is proved that she did intentionally fire the revolver by pointing it at the body of Stephen and so caused that bullet wound from which he died, she is guilty of murder. No feeling of regret, no feeling of pity, should deter you from doing the duty you have been called upon to do.

I think I ought to refer to something which Sir Percival Clarke said when he was opening the case. Counsel was perfectly right when he said that if a person was proved to have unlawfully killed another, the law presumed that killing to be murder until the contrary was shown. In my judgement that doctrine really only applies to a case where there is no evidence as to the intention of the person except the mere act. When you have evidence, as in this case—the evidence of the accused herself as to the circumstances in which the killing was done—it is better to invite you to decide the case on the evidence without reference to any legal doctrine at all.

The background of the picture which has been partly painted for your consideration is not a pleasant one. It is a story of two rather useless lives. It is a story of a young man of twenty-five, strong and healthy, who, at one time when he did any work, had been a dress designer—I suppose that means a lady's dress designer. For some time he lived on gifts from his parents and his brother, and finally descended to live in part at least on the private income of this woman. She is a young woman, aged twenty-six, the daughter of persons who, from the little evidence we have had in this case, appear to be of some position and evidently of considerable means.

She is educated, as you can tell from her speech in the witness box. She tells you she was married unhappily. It would not be right that we should form any opinion in this case as to whether the story of her married life which she told us is the truth or the whole truth. We are not trying her husband.

Although, as I gather, her parents' house was open to her, she chose to go and live, having some private income of her own, in this converted garage. On the ground floor was less a sitting room than a lounge, in the corner of which was a service counter called a 'cocktail bar'. Upstairs there was an unfurnished room; a bedroom which the prisoner occupied, often accompanied by the deceased man; and a bathroom.

In that flat she lived a life with the deceased man of a kind which would make one expect to find two things, and you find them in this case.

First, that between these two people there would be passion, devotion, and a sort of rather hysterical intimacy and affection such as is revealed in the two letters which you have heard read. There is no reason to doubt that the man was very fond of her; there is not the smallest reason to doubt that she was passionately devoted to him. It was an affection, however, based rather upon sexual matters than upon any real abiding love founded on mutual esteem. And the second sort of thing you might expect to happen under such circumstances is that there would be violent, passionate quarrels between these two people. Again you find it in this case.

The evidence of the neighbours seemed to indicate that Mrs Barney's flat was regarded as rather a nuisance in the mews, for they heard of, not one or two, but quite frequent occasions when there were rows and noises coming from there which woke people up in the night. You heard from police officers that there had been occasions when Mrs Barney had sent to the police station for the purpose of having some of her guest friends turned out in the middle of the night. They knew that the relations of these two people were such that on at least two occasions—one of them when the man died—the quarrel took the form of both of them shouting, the woman shouting and screaming out, and the man's voice also being raised. You can imagine the sort of life these persons were leading.

On 30 May, as on many previous dates, the prisoner and the deceased man spent the day together. The function was one of those cocktail parties attended by some thirty friends. It seems to have been perfectly orderly, but it was merely an incident in the case. After the party, at about eight o'clock in the evening, the two went to dine together with a young man-friend at a restuarant; there seemed to have been little accommodation for cooking at the mews. The prisoner paid the bill for herself and both her male companions. They went to a dance club and the two stayed there until about 12.30, when they went back to the flat, in the bedroom of which they intended to pass the night.

Somewhere about half-past four in the early morning—the time is not material—that revolver was discharged and the bullet entered the lung of the deceased man. How did it happen? Of direct evidence, there is absolutely none for the Prosecution; there can be none; and the circumstances of the case forbid that there should be any. The two persons were alone in the bedroom in the early hours of the morning; no one could see in; there was no one else on the premises; and the Prosecution ask you to say that what happened was that the prisoner deliberately shot and killed the deceased man because, first of all, of what was heard by people outside.

The witness who spoke most definitely about the matter was Mrs Hall. You saw her and might have formed the opinion that she was a sensible, quiet, composed person. She gave her evidence very clearly and was undoubtedly attempting to tell you the truth. She said that somewhere about four o'clock in the morning she heard 'rowing' going on at 21, which was about twenty yards away—the sort of rowing that had often been heard before coming from the same place. She said that the woman's voice was raised to a scream and that it was the voice of Mrs Barney. The man's voice was raised, too, and the noise was such that it woke her child. Mrs Hall said that she looked out of the window and heard Mrs Barney say: 'Get out; I will shoot, I will shoot.'

That is entirely a matter for you. It is a matter of common experience that persons who are awakened in the middle of the night by hearing loud voices coming from inside a room twenty yards away might very likely be mistaken as to the exact words that they heard. It would be asking too much of any person to ask that they should be absolutely reliable as to the exact words that they heard. The sense of what they heard, however, would appeal to the mind of any person. It is perfectly true, as Sir Patrick Hastings has pointed out, that Mrs Barney was not heard to say: 'Get out, I will shoot *you*.' Mrs Hall went on to say that after that she heard a shot, and then something like 'Good God, what have you done?' What had happened, as we all know, was that the man had been shot in the lung.

Mrs Hall obviously made a mistake in thinking that she heard Mrs Barney say the word 'Chicken', but 'Chicken' and 'Mickey' sound very much alike. What Mrs Barney said was probably: 'Mickey, come back to me. I will do everything I can for you.'

You have heard criticisms of the evidence of Mrs Stevens, who said that she heard what you all know did not happen in that mews. She was under the impression that she heard five shots, and you might think that, inasmuch as she clearly made a mistake about that, it would be unsafe and unfair in a criminal trial to rely to any extent at all on the evidence of this witness except so far as other people said the same thing.

Kiff, the chauffeur, who lived next door, said that he was

awakened by the row going on at the flat, and that he turned on the light and found that the time was 4.35. That was probably the time of the tragedy, for immediately afterwards he heard the shot.

The Crown next called a witness who ought not to be called '*the* witness for the Prosecution', but a person who was a perfectly independent gentleman and certainly not likely to be desirous of saying anything against his patient. He was properly called by the Prosecution because he was first on the scene and not because he helped to convict or to acquit. Dr Durrant described Mrs Barney as being overwrought, hysterical, babbling, almost crazy—all meaning much the same thing. One thing is clear, that her story was that of a struggle for the revolver between herself and her lover—her lover who was lying dead. Any woman was likely to be hysterical in such circumstances. From what she first said, she seemed to be rather reproachful that the doctor had not come earlier—that the dead man wanted to tell him that it was an accident and not her fault. Without doubting that the woman was telling the truth, it was the sort of thing a man might say and, if he had any decency in him, would say. Mrs Barney was obviously very devoted to the man and kissed the dead body in the doctor's presence. At that time she was desirous of killing herself, and the doctor thought it necessary to prevent her picking up the revolver. She said: 'Let me die. I want to kill myself.'

The doctor demanded from her an explanation of what had happened. That seems to be a matter of the most striking importance. It is perfectly true that one of the most useful pieces of evidence which is ever given in a criminal case is the statement of the accused person before he or she has had time to think very much, consider their position, or receive any advice, because in those circumstances you are likely to get the truth. Therefore, I do commend to you as being of the greatest importance the story which Mrs Barney told to Dr Durrant, and more particularly because he told us that it was not a cool, collected story, but that it was the result of his piecing together a series of somewhat incoherent, disjointed remarks by her.

According to the story she told to Dr Durrant, she was
threatening Stephen with what would happen if he left her—
not threatening that he would die, but that he would lose
her because she would commit suicide; that he then made a
dash for the chair and picked up this revolver which was
under a cushion, kept, as he knew, on that chair and fully
loaded.

If the prisoner's story of how she became possessed of that
revolver was true—and you ought to accept it because you
have had no other evidence about it for the purpose of the
case—then that person, Captain Coler, an officer in His
Majesty's service, who gave to a girl, who must have been
under twenty-one years of age at the time, that revolver and
nine or ten rounds of ammunition, any of which was sufficient
to kill a man, must be feeling a very unhappy man today.
It is astonishing that any person in a responsible position
should have been guilty of such an act of wicked negligence
as to give a revolver to a young woman like that without a
word of warning as to the danger of using it, the undesirability
of keeping it loaded, and without mentioning that she would
be incurring a substantial penalty and liable to be sent to
prison if she kept it without a police certificate, which
assuredly she would not have got.

The stories which Mrs Barney told to the police, and afterwards in the witness box, were almost identical. And to be
quite frank, what passed through my mind when I listened
to the final speeches was that it was not asked by counsel
what right they had to say that that story is untrue. Of course,
one must remember that it is a story told by the person who
has every motive for telling a story which will assist herself,
but Dr Durrant's view is that at the time when it was first
told, this woman was in such a state of wild excitement and
grief that she was quite incapable of making up a story with
no foundation in fact, and of telling it in a series of disjointed
sentences. If you accept his evidence, can you say that you put
aside as untrue altogether that story told by herself?

If the story is found to be inconsistent with the true facts
of the case then it will be your duty to examine it very
narrowly having regard to the source from which it comes.

But if the story is not inconsistent with the known facts of the case, to reject it would mean this—that you reject it because it is told by a person who is on her trial. If so, it does not seem to me that there is very much use in the Act of Parliament passed in 1898, which allowed accused persons to give evidence on their own behalf.

Unless you can find some sufficient grounds in this case for saying you decline to accept that story told to Dr Durrant, it seems to me that you will find considerable difficulty in saying that the Prosecution has proved that she did deliberately and intentionally shoot at this man with the intention of killing him.

However wrong, however wicked it might be to threaten to take her own life, it seems that the last thing she really desired or had in her mind at that time was the death of the man who was her lover.

She further told Dr Durrant that she had often had quarrels with this man and sometimes was terrified of him; that he had broken the kitchen window on one occasion and that she had had to call in the police. She told Dr Durrant that she had often felt inclined to commit suicide, and she gave him an explanation of a bullet mark which had scraped along the paper of the wall and ricocheted off the wall into the wardrobe. She told him that it was the mark of a bullet which she had fired some time ago when the deceased man had created a disturbance outside her flat; that she had asked him to go away and he had refused, and that to create an effect she had fired at random.

At this point the court adjourned for luncheon, the judge asking the jury not to discuss the matter among themselves at that stage, but to wait until he had finished his summing-up.

THE SUMMING-UP (*continued*):

The next person to come on the scene after Dr Durrant was Inspector Winter. He asked her about the revolver, and she said that it was hers and that she had had it a long time; that last night she and the deceased man had quarrelled, that he got the revolver from the chair, and that they struggled

and it went off. She added: 'It is terrible; leave me alone.'
It was a short statement, but much to the same effect as the
one she had made to Dr Durrant. At the police station she
said: 'I did not shoot him; I am not guilty.' Inspector Campion
produced the statement taken down in writing at the police
station. Describing the occurrence of that particular night
the prisoner, after referring to the events of the day, said:

Immediately we got in we had a quarrel about a woman
he was fond of. He knew I had a revolver in the house. I
have had it for years. I do not know where it came from. It
was kept in various places. Last night it was under the
cushion of a chair in the bedroom, near the bed. I was afraid
of it and I used to hide it from time to time. He knew where
it was last night. He took it from under the chair saying,
'I'm going to take it away for fear you will kill yourself.' He
went into the room on the left. I ran after him and tried to
get it back. There was no struggle in the bedroom. He was
outside in the spare room in the doorway. As we were struggling together—he wanted to take it away and I wanted to
get it back—it went off. Our hands were together, his hands
in mine . . .

Mr Churchill explained how it was that a cartridge
between two discharged ones had not been fired, and Sir
Patrick Hastings was eloquent in showing how there must
have been a struggle because there were no definite fingerprints on the revolver of the two persons concerned, only
confused fingerprints on and all over it.

Evidence would be admissible if it showed a previous
attempt, but it was also admissible to show that the prisoner
on some previous occasion had taken the loaded revolver in
her hand and discharged it in the course of a quarrel with
the deceased man and if she used words to indicate that she
was threatening to shoot. The evidence of Mrs Hall was
remarkable, not so much because it differed from the evidence
given by the accused woman, but because in so many
particulars she was corroborated by the accused, whose own
testimony showed that Mrs Hall was a very accurate woman.

She said that about three weeks before 30 May, early in the

H

morning, there was a row. There had been a disagreement about the damage done to a cab, and later she heard the prisoner screaming out of the window, telling the deceased to go away before she sent for the police. The man was at the door asking for money. He came in a taxi-cab and went away in it. Later, she saw him coming from the direction of the prisoner's flat, and she heard the prisoner say: 'Laugh, baby, laugh for the last time', and then she fired out of the window, holding the revolver in her left hand. The man was not hit and he went back and told Mrs Barney not to be so silly as everyone in the mews was looking. Mrs Barney, after firing the shot, fell down inside the flat as though she had fainted.

The prisoner agreed with almost all of that, but she said that although she fired the revolver on that occasion, she did not fire it out of the window. The words, 'Laugh, baby, laugh', might be indicative of the fact that she was firing at or near the deceased rather than at herself. Mrs Hall said that Mrs Barney fired with the revolver in her left hand, and if Sir Patrick Hastings had not asked the prisoner to lift the revolver when she was in the witness box, I would have done so; I had made a note to that effect. The prisoner used her right hand when she raised the weapon while she was in the witness box.

If the firing was for the purpose of frightening the man, and, as the prisoner said, 'to create an effect', and not a deliberate attempt to shoot him, the evidence of that occasion becomes insufficient; otherwise it is admissible. The prisoner herself admitted that she had uttered the words: 'Smile, baby, smile.'

On the other hand, if you accept the rest of Mrs Hall's evidence, declaring there was on that one occasion a great noise of squabbling, and think that the prisoner was angry and picked up the revolver and fired it, you may do so.

If the Prosecution ask you to say it was a deliberate attempt to kill a man at twenty yards off, I can say that if I were now trying that charge I should rule that the evidence in support of it was far too unsatisfactory to go to the jury.

On the facts relating to the events on the early morning of 31 May, you, the jury, will have to say whether the Prose-

cution has established first of all that it was the prisoner's
hand which made the revolver go off; secondly, that she
intentionally fired it; and thirdly, that when she fired it she
pointed at the deceased with the intention of killing him. If
you acquit her of murder, you will have to consider whether
she is guilty of the lesser crime of manslaughter. Counsel has
said nothing about manslaughter, and there is nothing they
could have said on the facts. The question of the law of manslaughter is for me to direct the jury upon. Manslaughter
consists in the unlawful killing of another person without
any intention of killing and without any intention of seriously
injuring that person.

A great legal authority, Serjeant Hawkins, had something
to say on the subject of manslaughter. His words were written
so long ago that the seventh edition of his book [*A Treatise of
the Pleas of the Crown*], which I hold in my hand, is dated
1795, but they are as true today as they were then. They
were:

> I direct you that if a person in the course of doing an act
> which is unlawful and dangerous causes the death of another,
> that person is guilty of manslaughter.

Applying that statement of law to the facts in this case, it
amounts to this: if the prisoner threatened to commit suicide
with that revolver on the early morning of 31 May, if Stephen
removed that revolver to prevent her committing that crime
—and attempting to commit suicide is a crime—and if she,
in order to carry out that intention, struggled with him and
caused the revolver to go off and kill him, although she had
no intention of killing or injuring him, she would be guilty
of manslaughter. I invite you to consider these three altern-
atives:

First, is she guilty or not of murder?

Second, is she guilty or not of manslaughter?

Third, and this will be your verdict, unless you are satisfied
that she is guilty of one or the other of the offences—that she
is not guilty of any offence at all.

The jury retired at 2.55 pm and returned at 4.47 pm.

VERDICT

CLERK OF THE COURT: Members of the jury, will your foreman please stand? Mr Foreman of the jury, are you agreed upon your verdict?

FOREMAN: We are.

CLERK: Do you find Elvira Dolores Barney guilty of murder?

FOREMAN: Not guilty.

CLERK: Do you find her guilty of manslaughter?

FOREMAN: Not guilty.

CLERK: And that is the verdict of you all?

FOREMAN: Yes.

FURTHER INDICTMENT

SIR PERCIVAL CLARKE *then referred to the further indictment that was on the file against* MRS BARNEY. *That indictment, he said, charged her with shooting at Stephen on 19 May with intent to murder him, or with intent to do him grievous bodily harm, and with common assault. It had been suggested that those charges had been used to bolster up a non-existent case, but they had been examined before a magistrate of considerable experience, and he had formed the opinion that there was a case to meet, and that opinion had been approved by the grand jury. At no time had the charge been thought of to bolster up a non-existent case. Having regard, however, to what his Lordship had said and to the fact that all the evidence had now been thoroughly examined and sifted, he* (SIR PERCIVAL CLARKE) *might be allowed to exercise his discretion, and he hoped that his Lordship would approve if he asked to have a verdict of 'Not Guilty' taken as regards those charges.*

MR JUSTICE HUMPHREYS *intimated that he fully approved of that course being taken.*

MRS BARNEY *was then formerly charged with regard to those matters. She pleaded 'Not Guilty', and, on his Lordship's direction, the jury acquitted her of those charges.*

APPENDICES

APPENDIX 1

Leading Dates

1905		Elvira Dolores Mullens born
1928 August	2	Elvira Mullens marries John Sterling Barney at Princes Row Register Office, London
1929 July	27	Elvira and John Barney separate
1931 January	1	Elvira Barney purchases lease of 21 Williams Mews
1932 May	30	Cocktail party held at 21 Williams Mews between 5.30 and 9 pm
	31	In the early hours Michael Scott Stephen is shot dead
June	3	Elvira Barney arrested and charged with the murder of Stephen
	6	Elvira Barney appears at Westminster Police Court and is remanded in custody
	13	At the end of the committal proceedings Mrs Barney is committed for trial
July	4	Trial begins at the Central Criminal Court, Old Bailey, before Mr Justice Humphreys
	6	Trial ends. Mrs Barney is acquitted on the two counts of murder and manslaughter
	23	Mrs Barney appears at Westminster Police Court to answer summons concerning illegal possession of a firearm, and is disqualified from holding firearms and fined
1936 December	25	Mrs Barney found dead in her Paris hotel
	27	After identifying their daughter's body, Sir John and Lady Mullens issue a statement to the press: 'We are quite satisfied that it is a case of natural death'

APPENDIX 2

From the *Star*, 7 July 1932:

MRS BARNEY: TODAY

Mrs Barney, looking much recovered, went for a motor ride today—skilfully driving a high-speed sports car.

She left her parents' house in Belgrave Square, W, in dramatic style just after noon.

All was quiet in the mews behind the house where the family cars are kept. Suddenly the double doors of the garage were flung open by a chauffeur in uniform.

There was heard the loud roar of the exhaust of a very powerful car. It was apparent that the engine and everything else had been got ready for a quick getaway.

Almost before the doors were open wide enough, there dashed into the mews a Delage sports car.

Mrs Barney, wearing a blue costume and a white knitted cap, was at the wheel. By her side was a young dark man wearing a grey suit.

As the car came into the mews, Mrs Barney, who was smiling, stamped on the brake, skidded round an acute left-hand turn, and raced out through the exit.

She braked again very hard as she passed under an archway, and spun the car round into Wilton Crescent.

Shortly before two o'clock Mrs Barney drove home to lunch.

As she rang the front door bell she was surrounded by photographers. In response to their request that she would smile, she did so broadly.

'I feel a lot better than yesterday. I am glad that the ordeal is over. My plans are not settled yet. Everybody has been most kind to me,' she said as she entered.

APPENDIX 3

From the *Sunday Dispatch*, 10 July 1932:

GREATER TRAGEDY
by Mrs Elvira Barney

I write in tears.

People think of me as an exotic woman who was on trial for her life.

They forget that my greater tragedy is with me yet.

The man I loved more than anything else in the world is dead, and now that I have come back to the freedom which I once shared with him, I am reminded in a thousand different ways of all that he meant to me.

I see again all those places in London where we used to be about together, I see the cinemas where he and I have been so often, I see the things that he used to like, the favourite walks we used to take in the parks, even the trees and the sunshine seem to belong to him.

It all makes me so despondent, all these memories bring me such a heartache that if I smile I am not conscious of doing so.

There is no spontaneous joy in my life. I force a smile when people tell me to cheer up, and add that I shall feel better as my health improves.

At the moment I am terribly distressed. Misunderstandings are constantly in the public mind.

People crowded round my parents' house, both at the back and front, and photographers waited for me, saying that they would stay there until I did come out.

Was I to stay in indefinitely, to deny myself the fresh air for which I had pined during the six weeks I had been locked up, or was I to face the crowd?

I decided to come out, and have done with all these crowds who were distressing my parents every bit as much as myself.

Someone asked me if I was not glad to be home. What an unnecessary question! Of course I was, and if it forced a smile to my lips it was no more than the reaction of any human being.

The photographers were quick to seize their chance. They made the most of their skill, but I am sure they would have spared me had they known the distress it has brought to us, with the flood of letters and abuse from people who do not know the circumstances of the episode at all.

'I LOVED HIM'

I loved Michael very, very much, but I suppose no one who has not been through my terrible ordeal can ever understand my feelings.

That great sigh of relief that I gave when first I realised I was free expressed a passing feeling.

Who could not be infinitely glad that a jury had believed one's word in a tragedy which had affected the whole course of one's life?

APPENDIX 4

From the *Spectator,* 16 July 1932:

A VICTORY FOR DECENCY

It has been stated that Mrs Elvira Barney has given to a Member of Parliament, who had put down a motion regarding her possession of a revolver, a written undertaking to refrain from writing any further articles for publication for twelve months, and to discontinue the series already begun. The Member in question, Mr G. G. Mitcheson, has explained that his sole purpose in putting the question was to do all in his power to stop such articles as have already begun to appear. He is to be congratulated both on his action and its result. Our strictures on what has already appeared in print are in no way affected by the promise he has secured, but the knowledge that his attitude is that of the overwhelming mass of self-respecting persons in this country encourages some dim hope that the Sunday Press may hesitate a little longer in the future before inviting this particular type of contribution to its columns.

APPENDIX 5

From the *Sunday Dispatch,* 17 July 1932:

MRS BARNEY'S ARTICLES

We regret to learn that Mrs Barney is so overwrought, as a result of the severe strain to which she was recently subjected, that her health has broken down and she has been advised by her doctor to take absolute and complete rest.

Mrs Barney's desire in writing an explanation of her past life was, we understand, to correct the misrepresentations which have been circulated regarding her.

In these circumstances, the *Sunday Dispatch,* which had

arranged to publish certain articles by her, at once expressed its willingness to release Mrs Barney from any obligation to write any further articles and arrangements to this end were completed last Tuesday.

We would add that Mrs Barney has refused to receive any remuneration for anything she has already written.

We feel sure our readers will join with us in expressing sympathy with her parents, Sir John and Lady Mullens.

APPENDIX 6

From the *Daily Mail*, 22 July 1932:

Mrs Elvira Dolores Barney, of Belgrave Square, S.W., was at Westminster yesterday fined by Mr Boyd £50, with £10 10s costs, for being in possession of a five-chambered revolver without a certificate.

She was recently acquitted at the Old Bailey on an indictment charging her with the murder of Mr 'Michael' Stephen, who was found shot in her flat at Williams Mews, Knightsbridge, S.W.

Mr Walker Frampton, who defended, pleaded guilty.

Mr E. Barker prosecuted, and during his speech Mrs Barney sobbed loudly, at times almost drowning his voice. He said that when the police went to her flat they found on the floor a five-chambered revolver. Two of the chambers had been discharged. Mrs Barney admitted it was her revolver, that she had had it for years, and that she had no licence.

'That is all I need say about the facts,' said Mr Barker. 'I submit that this is a bad case. This Act is directed against persons who are not fit and proper persons to have a licence. This young woman is totally unfit to have a revolver.

'I do not wish to say anything more. The revolver is in the possession of the police and is now confiscated, and I apply that it should not be handed over to her.'

REVOLVER A GIFT

Mr Frampton said Mrs Barney was before the magistrate on three occasions concerning an accident which happened owing to the possession of the revolver. He continued:

Mrs Barney is twenty-six and it was proved at the trial that she came into possession of this revolver as a gift some nine years ago. She was ignorant of the fact that she should have taken out a certificate.

Unfortunately a fatal accident happened. The circumstances attending that accident have been fully investigated and it has been ascertained that it was an accident.

That result having been arrived at on 6 July, on 13 July this summons was applied for. Had there been no accident you would have felt bound to do no more than impose a pecuniary penalty.

Neither you nor anybody else who has not gone through that experience can conceive the agony and anguish of five weeks in Holloway awaiting trial for murder. Has she not been sufficiently punished already?

Mrs Barney throughout the whole time she was waiting her trial was in a serious condition of health. Since the trial she has also been attended by Dr Durrant, Sir James Purves-Stewart, and another medical man, and arrangements have been completed so that she will have prolonged and proper treatment.

Mrs Barney's sobs continued to punctuate counsel's speech, and reaching out from her chair she grasped one of the side supports of the dock and leaned her head upon her outstretched arms.

'My submission,' said Mr Frampton, 'is that you have before you a woman who has undergone a terrible ordeal, and I ask you to treat it as a case of a person ignorant of the law.'

UNFIT FOR FIREARMS

Mr Boyd (the magistrate) in giving his decision, said: 'It would have been wrong if these proceedings had not been taken, and it would have been quite impossible for anything to be done in this matter until the very grave charges had been dealt with.

'I think it is abundantly shown that if she had in fact applied for a certificate it would have been quite impossible for anyone to have granted it. Apart from any other consideration, she was a person quite unfitted to possess a firearm.

'The happenings which resulted in the arrest of Mrs Barney and her trial would never have occurred had she not been guilty of unlawful possession of a revolver.

'I have no hesitation in describing this as a bad case, and I can see no redeeming feature in it. I should regard this case as one for both fine and imprisonment were it not for the facts which you, Mr Frampton, have very properly introduced into your observations.'

At this point Mrs Barney broke down completely. She sat doubled up in her chair, and her sobs echoed throughout the court.

CARRIED FROM COURT

'Mrs Barney was in custody from the day of her arrest until the jury acquitted her on very, very grave charges,' concluded Mr Boyd. 'In these circumstances only I feel it is not a case in which I should make it part of the sentence that she should go to prison for a second time, for that is what it would mean. But there must be a substantial fine of £50, with £10 10s costs.'

On hearing the decision Mrs Barney collapsed. Inspector Winter rushed forward and caught her as she swayed in her chair, and with the help of another officer lifted her to her feet, and half carried her out of the court.

Later she drove away alone in a taxicab from a back gate of the police station.

APPENDIX 7

From the *Morning Post*, 31 August 1932:

TRAGEDY OF DRUGS AND DEPRESSION

INQUEST VERDICT ON MRS GAMBLE

UNCONQUERABLE HABIT

MYSTERIOUS REFERENCES IN LAST NOTE

The tragic death of Mrs Gertrude Gamble, aged 42, who fell from a window of a hotel in Half Moon Street, Piccadilly, W. on Friday night, was investigated by Mr Ingleby Oddie at Westminster yesterday, and a verdict that she committed suicide 'through this unconquerable habit of taking drugs, and while of unsound mind,' was recorded.

Mr S. Coleman, Mr C. Gordon Thompson, and Mr J. C. M. Easton represented interested parties.

Sir John Mullens, father of Mrs Elvira Barney, was present at the court.

In summing up, the Coroner said: 'Not only does Mrs Gamble's history suggest very strongly that this was suicide, but she has made a previous attempt on her life, the motive then being much the same as the motive now—drug taking and debt and general depression.

'She has left a letter. She evidently contemplated taking her life because she had torn up the rest of her correspondence except this letter and a note, addressed to her landlady.

'In the letter which was was found in her pocket she says: "Dear Mrs Urban, I am very sorry to bring this further trouble on you, but I am too unhappy and lonely to go on. Tom Chadbourne and Elvira Barney are responsible for this. Please ask the police to communicate with Mrs Morris, St Leonards-on-Sea, my only relative, and please make Mullens pay the account. I am so unhappy. Yours V. E. Graham. My real name is Gamble."'

The Coroner said that the word 'make' in the letter was underlined.

'I have spoken to the representative of Sir John Mullens and Mrs Barney,' added Mr Oddie, 'and as he does not think it necessary for them to appear to explain what this reference to them means I do not propose to adjourn the inquest.'

APPENDIX 8

From *The Daily Telegraph*, 10 October 1933:

MRS ELVIRA BARNEY DIVORCED

LONDON TRIAL EVIDENCE

From our own correspondent

NEW YORK, Monday

Mrs Elvira Barney has been divorced here by her husband, Mr John Sterling Barney, the American singer. The ground for the divorce was evidence given in London at the trial of Mrs Barney on a charge of shooting Thomas William Scott Stephen, of which she was acquitted.

The marriage took place in August 1929. But, Mr Barney states, they soon separated, and he has been in the United States for the greater part of the last few years.

The charge of shooting, on which Mrs Barney who is 26, was

acquitted, arose out of the discovery of the young man, Scott Stephen, lying dead in her flat at Knightsbridge in 1932.

A few months later a collision occurred on the Riviera between her car and that of Countess Karolyi, in which the countess was injured. Mrs Barney was fined a small sum.

APPENDIX 9

From the *Sunday Dispatch,* 27 December 1936:

SHE TRIED IN VAIN TO FORGET THE PAST

From a Special Correspondent

Since her acquittal, Elvira Barney spent her time between London and Paris. She lived in West End hotels and later in a Belgravia flat.

The trial left its mark on her. Although still young, she looked middle-aged.

She tried to get work.

'I am fed up with doing nothing,' she told me when I met her at a West End night club. 'I could do with the money.

'I want so much to forget all that happened, but I am never allowed to. Wherever I go I feel that people are looking at me and talking about me.

'The only people who want to know me now seem to be the type of person who wants to be seen with the "notorious Mrs Barney."

'I am reconciled to the fact that I will never be really happy again. That is why I want a job that will help me to forget.

'I used to think I could kill the past by getting around and having a good time, but it just didn't work out.

'I am tired of clubs and parties. I just want a chance to settle down and live a reasonable life.

'At present I am thinking of going into a flower shop, but I rather doubt whether it will come to anything.'

I asked her whether the rumours that she was to marry were true. She said she had considered remarriage.

'But I have a feeling that my hoodoo will step in again. I somehow feel that I'm not fated to be happy,' she said with tears in her eyes.

APPENDIX 10

From the *Daily Mirror*, 28 December 1936:

MOTHER DENIES MRS BARNEY WAS ENGAGED TO WED

By a special correspondent

In the slow tones of one mastering grief with difficulty, Lady Mullens, mother of *Mrs Elvira Dolores Barney*, yesterday denied the engagement report current since *Mrs Barney was found dead in a Paris hotel on Christmas Day*.

Mrs Barney, who in 1932 was acquitted on a charge of murder, had spent Christmas Eve in a tour of the gay cafés and restaurants of Montmartre, Montparnasse and the Latin Quarter.

On receiving news of her death her parents—Sir John Mullens, formerly the Government Stockbroker, and Lady Mullens—at once went to Paris.

Lady Mullens told me last night: 'We are quite satisfied that it is a case of natural death.

'The story that our daughter was going to marry again is not correct. Many absurd stories have been told.'

When Sir John and Lady Mullens arrived in Paris they hurried to the hotel, but Sir John waited in the hall while his wife went up to the room in which their daughter lay dead.

M. René Jean Cady, to whom Mrs Barney was reported to be engaged, said last night:

'Our marriage was not yet decided on, but we talked about it. Her death came as a great shock to me. She had been very worried lately.'

Cady, well-known to most of the Paris night clubs and bars, is a tall, blond, good-looking boy, and claims to be descended from the royal family of D'Orleans.

Mrs Barney was only thirty-one.

ACKNOWLEDGEMENTS

The account in this book of the trial of Elvira Barney is compiled from unofficial as well as official sources. I wish to acknowledge the assistance I have received from the following: Cyril Arthur; Harold Atkins; Nicolas Bentley; Weston Drury; Lady Gardiner; Bruce Hollingsworth; Lord Kinross; Mrs Effie Leigh; William McIlroy; Mrs Ruby Milton; Hobe Morrison; Beverley Nichols; F. A. Normanton; Charles Rodda; Miss Beatrix Thomson; Mrs Dorothy Turner-Valdan and Patrick Waddington.

In writing this book, I have quoted such comments as seemed helpful from the press of over 40 years ago. Some of the proprietors and editors, with their publications, are beyond my felicitations, but to those who survive I make my acknowledgements.

My thanks are due also to the following publishers and the writers concerned: Wm Heinemann Ltd for permission to quote from *The Autobiography of Sir Patrick Hastings*; George Harrap & Co for permission to quote from *The Other Mr Churchill* by Macdonald Hastings; Allan Wingate Ltd for permission to quote from *Defender's Triumph* by Edgar Lustgarten; Batsford Ltd for permission to quote from *The Thirties* by Julian Symons; and Victor Gollancz Ltd for permission to quote from *Living Twice* by C. H. Rolph.

Finally, warm appreciation goes to my mother, Mrs Rose Boulting, who has helped to recall memories; Graham Ashley for typing the manuscript; Harry Brown of the Press Association for providing facilities and personal assistance; Louisa Pipe and Pipe-Rich (Angel Studio) for their ready cooperation in taking so many photographs for the sake of one; and, last but not least, my thanks to Jonathan Goodman for practical encouragement in the writing of this book.